CONTENTS

2001 KNOCK-KNOCKS
&
TONGUE TWISTERS

By Mike Artell, Ronny M. Cole, Charles Keller,
Joseph Rosenbloom & Chris Tait

Main Street
A division of Sterling Publishing Co., Inc.
New York

Library of Congress Cataloging-in-Publication Data Available

2 4 6 8 10 9 7 5 3 1

Published by Sterling Publishing Co., Inc.
387 Park Avenue South, New York, NY 10016
Material in this collection was adapted from:
Giant Book of Knock-Knock Jokes © Joseph Rosenbloom & Ronny M. Cole
Best Knock-Knocks Book Ever © Charles Keller
Little Giant Book of Tongue Twisters © Mike Artell & Joseph Rosenbloom
Ridiculous Tongue Twisters © Chris Tait

Edited by Christine Byrnes
Design by Carmine Raspaolo
Cover Design by Alan Carr

© 2004 by Sterling Publishing Co., Inc.
Distributed in Canada by Sterling Publishing
c/o Canadian Manda Group, One Atlantic Avenue, Suite 105
Toronto, Ontario, Canada M6K 3E7
Distributed in Great Britain and Europe by Chris Lloyd at Orca Book
Services, Stanley House, Fleets Lane, Poole BH15 3AJ, England
Distributed in Australia by Capricorn Link (Australia) Pty. Ltd.
P.O. Box 704, Windsor, NSW 2756, Australia

Sterling ISBN 1-4027-1534-X

KNOCK-KNOCKS

Knock–knock.

Who's there?
Aardvark.
Aardvark who?
Aardvark-um cleaner broke.
Can I borrow yours?

Knock–knock.

Who's there?
Aaron.
Aaron who?
Aaron all the way home.

Knock–knock.

Who's there?
Aaron.
Aaron who?
Why Aaron you opening
the door?

Knock–knock.

Who's there?
Abbey.
Abbey who?
Abbey Birthday!

Knock–knock.

Who's there?
Abbot.
Abbot who?
Abbot time we eat, isn't it?

Knock–knock.

Who's there?
Abe.
Abe who?
Abe out face!

Knock–knock.

Who's there?
Abe Lincoln.
Abe Lincoln who?
Abe Lincoln break in the strongest chain.

Knock–knock.

Who's there?
Abe Lincoln.
Abe Lincoln who?
Abe Lincoln (a blinkin') yellow light means slow down!

Knock–knock.

Who's there?
Abercrombie.
Abercrombie who?
Abercrombie (have a crumby) time at the party!

Knock–knock.

Who's there?
Abyssinia.
Abyssinia who?
Abyssinia at the mall!

Knock–knock.

Who's there?
A.C.
A.C. who?
A.C. come and A.C. go.

Knock–knock.

Who's there?
Acey Ducey.
Acey Ducey who?
Acey your point, Ducey mine?

Knock–knock.

Who's there?
Adam.
Adam who?
Adam my way–
I'm coming in!

Knock–knock.

Who's there?
Achilles.
Achilles who?
Achilles mosquitoes with
a swatter! (Slap!)

Knock–knock.

Who's there?
Ada.
Ada who?
You're Ada your mind.

Knock–knock.

Who's there?
Adam.
Adam who?
Adam up and give me the bill.

Knock–knock.

Who's there?
Addison.
Addison who?
Addison no way to treat
an old friend.

Knock–knock.

Who's there?
Adore.
Adore who?
Adore is between us.

Knock–knock.

Who's there?
A.E.
A.E. who?
A.E. I owe you.

Knock–knock.

Who's there?
Afghan.
Afghan who?
Afghan away and never see you again.

Knock–knock.

Who's there?
Afghanistan.
Afghanistan who?
Afghanistan out here all night
if you don't open the door.

Knock–knock.

Who's there?
Agate.
Agate who?
Agate you covered!

Knock–knock.

Who's there?
Aiken.
Aiken who?
Oh, my Aiken back!

Knock–knock.

Who's there?
Aikido.
Aikido who?
Aikido you not.

Knock–knock.

Who's there?
A la mode.
A la mode who?
Remember the
A la mode (Alamo)!

Knock–knock.

Who's there?
Al and Edith.
Al and Edith who?
"Al and Edith love . . ."

Knock–knock.

Who's there?
Alaska.
Alaska who?
Alaska and you ask him.

Knock–knock.

Who's there?
Albee.
Albee who?
Albee a monkey's uncle!

Knock–knock.

Who's there?
Alcott.
Alcott who?
Alcott the cake.
You pour the tea.

Knock–knock.

Who's there?
Alda.
Alda who?
Alda time you knew who it was!

Knock–knock.

Who's there?
Alda and Alda.
Alda and Alda who?
I'm getting Alda and
Alda standing out here
in the cold.

Knock–knock.

Who's there?
Aldo.
Aldo who?
Aldo anything for you.

Knock–knock.

Who's there?
Aldous.
Aldous who?
Aldous fuss over little ol' me?

Knock–knock.

Who's there?
Aldous.
Aldous who?
Aldous knocking is giving me
a headache.

Knock–knock.

Who's there?
Aldus.
Aldus who?
Aldus talk and no action!

Knock–knock.

Who's there?
Alec.
Alec who?
Alec-tricity. Isn't that a shock?

Knock–knock.

Who's there?
Alex.
Alex who?
Alex the questions around here.

Knock–knock.

Who's there?
Alex.
Alex who?
Alex-plain later. Open the door.

Knock–knock.

Who's there?
Alfalfa.
Alfalfa who?
Alfalfa (I'll fall for) you, if you blow in my ear.

Knock–knock.

Who's there?
Ali.
Ali who?
Ali time you knew it was me.

Knock–knock.

Who's there?
Alfie.
　Alfie who?
Alfie you in my dreams.

Knock–knock.

　Who's there?
Alfie.
　　Alfie who?
Alfie-give your rudeness—I know
you're just being yourself.

Knock–knock.

Who's there?
Alfreda.
　Alfreda who?
Alfreda the dark.

Knock–knock.

　Who's there?
Alice.
　　Alice who?
Alice fair in love and war!

Knock–knock.

Who's there?
Alistair.
　Alistar who?
You uncover the pot, Alistair
the soup!

Knock–knock.

Who's there?
Alma.
   Alma who?
The dog ate Alma homework!

Knock–knock.

Who's there?
Alma Gibbons.
   Alma Gibbons who?
Alma Gibbons you 24 hours
to get out of town.

Knock–knock.

Who's there?
Aloha.
   Aloha who?
Aloha, there!

Knock–knock.

Who's there?
Althea.
   Althea who?
Althea in jail!

Knock–knock.

Who's there?
Altoona.
Altoona who?
Altoona piano—you play it!

Knock–knock.

Who's there?
Alva and Alma.
Alva and Alma who?
Alva day long I spend
Alma time outside your door.

Knock–knock.

Who's there?
Alyce.
Alyce who?
Alyce thought you
were nuts.

Knock–knock.

Who's there?
Amahl.
Amahl who?
Amahl tied up, call me later!

Knock–knock.

Who's there?
Amana.
Amana who?
Amana-eating tiger!

Knock–knock.

Who's there?
Amanda Lynn.
Amanda Lynn who?
Amanda Lynn player.

Knock–knock.

Who's there?
Amarillo.
Amarillo who?
Amarillo-fashioned girl.

Knock–knock.

Who's there?
Amarillo.
Amarillo who?
Amarillo nice guy.

Knock–knock.

Who's there?
Amateur.
Amateur who?
Amateur service.

Knock–knock.

Who's there?
Amaryllis.

Amaryllis who?
Amaryllis-state agent.
Want to buy a house?

Knock–knock.

Who's there?
Amerigo.

Amerigo who?
Amerigo-round.

Knock–knock.

Who's there?
Amen.

Amen who?
Amen hot water again.

Knock–knock.

Who's there?
Amish.

Amish who?
Amish you sho mush!

Knock–knock.

Who's there?
Amnesia.

Amnesia who?
Oh, I see you have it, too!

Knock–knock.

Who's there?
Amoeba.

Amoeba who?
"Amoeba wrong,
but I think you're
wonderful . . ."

Knock–knock.

Who's there?
Anastasia.

Anastasia who?
Anastasia out here
in the rain.

Knock–knock.

Who's there?
Anatol.

Anatol who?
Anatol you what
I thought of you.

Knock–knock.

Who's there?
Andalusia.

Andalusia who?
I'd like to take you someplace
Andalusia.

Knock–knock.

Who's there?
Andante.
Andante who?
I'm going to visit my uncle Andante too.

Knock–knock.

Who's there?
Andy.
Andy who?
Andy all lived happily ever after.

Knock–knock.

Who's there?
Andy.
Andy who?
Andy music goes on and on.

Knock–knock.

Who's there?
Andy Green.
Andy Greeen who?
"Andy Green grass grows all around,
all around . . ."

Knock–knock.

Who's there?
Angela.
Angela who?
Angela Mercy.

Knock–knock.

Who's there?
Anita.
Anita who?
Anita rest!

Knock–knock.

Who's there?
Anita.
Anita who?
Anita you like Anita hole in the head.

Knock–knock.

Who's there?
Anita.
Anita who?
Anita ride into town.

... THAT'S GOTTA HURT !!

Knock–knock.

Who's there?
Anna Mary.
Anna Mary who?
"Anna Mary old soul was he . . ."

Knock–knock.

Who's there?
Anna Maria Alberghetti.
    Anna Maria Alberghetti
    who?
"Anna Maria Alberghetti in
a taxi, honey . . . "

Knock–knock.

Who's there?
Annapolis.
    Annapolis who?
Annapolis day keeps the doctor away.

Knock–knock.

Who's there?
Annie.
    Annie who?
Annie-body alive in there?

Knock–knock.

Who's there?
Antilles.
    Antilles who?
Antilles open the door,
I'm gonna sit here on
your doorstep!

Knock–knock.

Who's there?
Anvil.
    Anvil who?
Anvil you be coming too?

Dracula:	**Knock–knock.**
Victim:	Who's there?
Dracula:	A-One.
Victim:	A-One who?
Dracula:	A-One to drink your blood.

Knock–knock.

   Who's there?
Apollo.
   Apollo who?
Any Apollo yours is Apollo mine.

Knock–knock.

  Who's there?
Apricot.
   Apricot who?
Apricot my key, open up.

Knock–knock.

   Who's there?
A quorum.
   A quorum who?
A quorum is where I keep my fish.

Knock–knock.

Who's there?
Archer.
Archer who?
Archer glad to see me?

Knock–knock.

Who's there?
Arlo.
Arlo who?
Arlo prices can't be beat.

Knock–knock.

Who's there?
Ariel.
Ariel who?
You're Ariel pain in the neck!

Knock–knock.

Who's there?
Arcudi.
Arcudi who?
Arcudi little dog can do one trick.

Knock–knock.

Who's there?
Arizona.
Arizona who?
Arizona room for one of us in this town.

Knock–knock.

Who's there?
Armada.

Armada who?
Armada told us there'd be
days like this.

Knock–knock.

Who's there?
Arm.

Arm who?
Arm always chasing rainbows.

Knock–knock.

Who's there?
Armand.

Armand who?
Armand the outside looking
inside.

Knock–knock.

Who's there?
Armstrong.

Armstrong who?
Armstrong as an ox—
and you have the brain of one.

...HE'S STRONG!...
NO BULL!

Knock–knock.

Who's there?
Arne.
Arne who?
Arne you going to ask me in?

Knock–knock.

Who's there?
Arno.
Arno who?
Arno kids to play with, so I'm bored.

Knock–knock.

Who's there?
Arsenio Hall.
Arsenio Hall who?
Arsenio Hall (I've seen you all) over town!

Knock–knock.

Who's there?
Artichoke.
Artichoke who?
Artichoke on a chicken bone.

Knock–knock.

Who's there?
Artie Fish.
Artie Fish who?
Artie Fish-el intelligence!

Knock–knock.

Who's there?
Aruba.
Aruba who?
Aruba (are you the) one in charge?

Knock–knock.

Who's there?
Aruba.
Aruba who?
Aruba your back, you rub'a mine.

Knock–knock.

Who's there?
Asbestos.
Asbestos who?
I'm doing Asbestos I can!

Knock–knock.

Who's there?
Ash.
Ash who?
Bless you.

Knock–knock.

Who's there?
Ashley.
Ashley who?
Ashley, I'm not sure . . .

Knock–knock.

Who's there?
Ashur.
Ashur who?
Ashur wish you'd
open this door.

Knock–knock.

Who's there?
Asparagus.
Asparagus who?
Asparagus the argument, we don't want to hear it.

Knock–knock.

Who's there?
Asta.
Asta who?
Asta La Veesta, baby!

Knock–knock.

Who's there?
Asthma.
Asthma who?
Asthma no questions.

Knock–knock.

Who's there?
Attila.
Attila who?
Attila no lies.

Knock–knock.

Who's there?
Astor.
Astor who?
Astor what her name is.

Knock–knock.

Who's there?
Astoria.
Astoria who?
I've got Astoria wouldn't believe!

Knock–knock.

Who's there?
Boris.
Boris who?
Go ahead, Boris with another story!

Knock–knock.

Who's there?
Atlas.
Atlas who?
Atlas I'm here.

Knock–knock.

Who's there?
Attila.
Attila who?
Attila we meet again!

Knock–knock.

Who's there?
Atwood.
    Atwood who?
Atwood be nice if you asked me in.

Knock–knock.

Who's there?
Aubrey.
    Aubrey who?
Aubrey Quiet!

Knock–knock.

Who's there?
Auerbach.
    Auerbach who?
Please scratch Auerbach.

Knock–knock.

Who's there?
Aunt Lou.
    Aunt Lou who?
Aunt Lou do you think you are?

Knock–knock.

Who's there?
Autumn.
    Autumn who?
You Autumn mind your own business!

Knock–knock.

Who's there?
Ava.
Ava who?
Ava seen you
someplace before?

Knock–knock.

Who's there?
Avenue.
Avenue who?
Avenue been missing me?

Knock–knock.

Who's there?
Avenue.
Avenue who?
Avenue heard the good news?

Knock–knock.

Who's there?
Avis.
Avis who?
Avis just at the zoo
and thought about you.

Knock–knock.

Who's there?
Avenue.
Avenue who?
Avenue heard this joke before?

Knock–knock.

Who's there?
Avocado.
Avocado who?
Avocado cold. Thad's why I dalk dis way.

Knock–knock.

Who's there?
Avon.
Avon who?
Avon to be alone.

Knock–knock.

Who's there?
Babbit.
    Babbit who?
Babbit and Costello!

Knock–knock.

Who's there?
Babylon.
    Babylon who?
Babylon—I'm not listening anyway!

Knock–knock.

Who's there?
Bach.
    Bach who?
Bach to the future!

Knock–knock.

Who's there?
Bacilli.
    Bacilli who?
Don't bacilli!

Knock–knock.

Who's there?
Baldoni.
Baldoni who?
Baldoni a little on the top.

Knock–knock.

Who's there?
Banana.
Banana who?
Banana messages for me?

Knock–knock.

Who's there?
Barbara.
Barbara who?
The Barbara Seville.

Knock–knock.

Who's there?
Barbara.
Barbara who?
"Barbara black sheep, have
you any wool . . ."

Knock–knock.

Who's there?
Barbie.
Barbie who?
Barbie Q. Chicken.

Knock–knock.

Who's there?
B.C.
B.C. who?
B.C'ing you!

Knock–knock.

Who's there?
Bea.
Bea who?
Bea Faroni!

Knock–knock.

Who's there?
Beecher.
Beecher who?
Beecher at any game you pick.

Knock–knock.

Who's there?
Beehive.
Beehive who?
Beehive yourself!

Knock–knock.

Who's there?
Bella.
Bella who?
Bella bottom trousers.

Knock–knock.

Who's there?
Belladonna.
Belladonna who?
Belladonna work, so I had
to knock.

Knock–knock.

Who's there?
Bella.
Bella who?
Bella the ball.

Knock–knock.

Who's there?
Belle Lee.
Belle Lee who?
Belle Lee Dancer.

Knock–knock.

Who's there?
Ben and Anna.
Ben and Anna who?
Ben and Anna split
so ice creamed.

Knock–knock.

Who's there?
Benny.
Benny who?
Benny long time no see.

Knock–knock.

Who's there?
Ben and Don.
Ben and Don who?
Ben there, Don that.

Knock–knock.

Who's there?
Bernie D.
Bernie D who?
Bernie D candles at both ends.

Knock–knock.

Who's there?
Beryl.
Beryl who?
Beryl of monkeys.

Knock–knock.

Who's there?
Bertha.
Bertha who?
Bertha-day greetings.

Knock–knock.

Who's there?
Bertha.
Bertha who?
Bertha the blues.

Knock–knock.

Who's there?
Beth.
Beth who?
Beth wisheth, thweetie.

Knock–knock.

Who's there?
Betty.
Betty who?
Betty-Bye!

Knock–knock.

Who's there?
Betty.
Betty who?
Betty B. Careful!

Knock–knock.

Who's there:
Bette.
Bette who?
Bette you can't guess my name.

Knock–knock.

Who's there?
Blake.
Blake who?
Blake a leg!

Knock–knock.

Who's there?
Blubber.
Blubber who?
"Blubber, come back to me . . ."

Knock–knock.

Who's there?
Blank.
Blank who?
You're welcome.

Knock–knock.

Who's there?
Blast.
Blast who?
Blast, but not least.

2001 Knock–Knocks & Tongue Twisters

Knock–knock.

Who's there?
Bob Dwyer.
Bob Dwyer who?
Bob Dwyer out here.
Caught my pants on it.

Knock–knock.

Who's there?
Apache.
Apache who?
Apache them for you.

Knock–knock.

Who's there?
Boise.
Boise who?
Boise strange!

Knock–knock.

Who's there?
Idaho.
Idaho who?
Idaho. I've seen stranger.

B

Knock–knock.

Who's there?
Bolivia.
Bolivia who?
Bolivia me!

Knock–knock.

Who's there?
Boll weevil.
Boll weevil who?
After the boll weevil all
go home.

Knock–knock.

Who's there?
Booty.
Booty who?
Booty is only skin deep.

Knock–knock.

Who's there?
Brighton.
Brighton who?
Up Brighton early
just to see you.

Knock–knock.

Who's there?
Brigham.
Brigham who?
Brigham a present!

Knock–knock.

Who's there?
Brinckerhoff.
Brinckerhoff who?
You Brinckerhoff the soda—
I'll bring the other half.

Knock–knock.

Who's there?
Britches.
Britches who?
"London Britches falling
down . . ."

Knock–knock.

Who's there?
Bruno.
Bruno who?
Bruno who it is!

Knock–knock.

Who's there?
Buck and Ham.
Buck and Ham who?
Buck and Ham Palace!

Knock–knock.

Who's there?
Budapest.
Budapest who?
You're nothing Budapest.

Knock–knock.

Who's there?
Buck.
Buck who?
"Buck, buck!" I'm a chicken.

Knock–knock.

Who's there?
Adelaide.
Adelaide who?
Adelaide an egg.

Knock–knock.

Who's there?
Eggs.
Eggs who?
Eggs-tremely cold out here in the chicken house.

Knock–knock.

Who's there?
Button.
Button who?
Button into what's not your business.

Knock–knock.

Who's there?
Butcher.
Butcher who?
"Butcher head on my shoulder . . ."

Knock–knock.

Who's there?
Caesar.
Caesar who?
"Caesar jolly good fellow . . ."

Knock–knock.

Who's there?
Cain and Abel.
Cain and Abel who?
Cain talk now–
Abel tomorrow.

Knock–knock.

Who's there?
Cain.
Cain who?
Cain you hear me?
Knock–knock!

Knock–knock.

Who's there?
Calder.
Calder who?
Calder police–
I've been robbed!

Knock–knock.

Who's there?
Camellia.
Camellia who?
Camellia little closer.

Knock–knock.

Who's there?
Cameron.
Cameron who?
Cameron over here.

Knock–knock.

Who's there?
Candace.
Candace who.
Candace door be opened?

Knock–knock.

Who's there?
Candace.
Candace who?
Candace snake do push-ups?

Knock–knock.

Who's there?
Candice.
Candice who?
Candice be love?

Knock–knock.

Who's there?
Cannibal.
Cannibal who?
Cannibal-eve you're for real!

Knock–knock.

Who's there?
Cannibal.
Cannibal who?
Cannibal (can a bull) ice skate?

Knock–knock.

Who's there?
Canoe.
Canoe who?
Canoe help me with my homework?

Knock–knock.

Who's there?
Cantaloupe.
Cantaloupe who?
Cantaloupe today,
maybe tomorrow . . .

Knock–knock.

Who's there?
Cantillo.
Cantillo who?
Cantillo my name,
but my face will be familiar.

Knock–knock.

Who's there?
Carew.
Carew who?
The Carew of the
Love Boat.

Knock–knock.

Who's there?
Caribbean.
Caribbean who?
You don't Caribbean
that I'm standing out
here in a snowstorm.

Knock–knock.

Who's there?
Canoe.
Canoe who?
Canoe please
get off my foot?

Knock–knock.

Who's there?
Carina.
Carina who?
Carina ditch. Can I
use your phone?

Knock–knock.

Who's there?
Carlo.
Carlo who?
Carlo on gas.

Knock–knock.

Who's there?
Carmen.
Carmen who?
"Carmen to my parlor,"
said the spider to the fly!

Knock–knock.

Who's there?
Carmen or Cohen.
Carmen or Cohen who?
You don't know whether you're Carmen or Cohen.

Knock–knock.

Who's there?
Carrie.
Carrie who?
Carrie R. Pigeon.

Knock–knock.

Who's there?
Carrie.
Carrie who?
Carrie me inside–
I'm tired.

Knock–knock.

Who's there?
Casanova.
Casanova who?
Casanova (isn't over) until the fat lady sings.

Knock–knock.

Who's there?
Cashew.
Cashew who?
Cashew see I'm busy?

Knock–knock.

Who's there?
Cashew.
Cashew who?
Cashew see it's me?

Knock–knock.

Who's there?
Casino.
Casino who?
Casino evil.

Knock–knock.

Who's there?
Carmencita.
Carmencita who?
Carmencita down and take
a load off your feet.

Knock–knock.

Who's there?
Cass.
Cass who?
Cass Toff, we're leaving!

Knock–knock.

Who's there?
Cassie.
Cassie who?
Cassie Nova!
How can you resist me?

Knock–knock.

Who's there?
Castanet.
Castanet who?
Castanet in the water to catch fish.

Knock–knock.

Who's there?
Cassie.
    Cassie who?
Cassie O. Watch!

Knock–knock.

Who's there?
Cassie.
    Cassie who?
Cassie you know–
I've got to run!

Knock–knock.

Who's there?
Cassius.
    Cassius who?
Cassius if you can!

Knock–knock.

Who's there?
C.D.
    C.D. who?
C.D. forest for the trees.

Knock–knock.

Who's there?
Cecilius.
    Cecilius who?
Cecilius Knock–Knock joke
I ever heard.

Knock–knock.

Who's there?
Celeste.
    Celeste who?
Celeste time I saw a face like
yours, I threw it a fish.

Knock–knock.

Who's there?
Cattle Drive.
Cattle Drive who?
This Cattle (cat will)
Drive you crazy!

Knock–knock.

Who's there?
Celeste.
Celeste who?
Celeste you know
the better!

Knock–knock.

Who's there?
Celia.
Celia who?
Celia later, alligator!

Knock–knock.

Who's there?
Censure.
Censure who?
Censure letters by first-class
mail.

Knock–knock.

Who's there?
Cereal.
Cereal who?
Cereal McCoy.

Knock–knock.

Who's there?
Chantelle.
Chantelle who?
Chantelle you anything.

Knock–knock.

Who's there?
Charlotta.
Charlotta who?
Charlotta fuss about nothing.

Knock–knock.

Who's there?
Checker.
Checker who?
Checker out.

Knock–knock.

Who's there?
Cheese.
Chesse who?
Cheese funny that way.

Knock–knock.

Who's there?
Cher.
Cher who?
Cher-lock Holmes.

Knock–knock.

Who's there?
Cher.
Cher who?
Cher would be nice
if you opened the door!

Knock–knock.

Who's there?
Cheese.
Cheese who?
Cheese a cute girl.

Knock–knock.

Who's there?
Cherry.
Cherry who?
Cherry Lewis!

Knock–knock.

Who's there?
Chesapeake.
Chesapeake who?
Chesapeake to me and I'll tell you everything.

Knock–knock.

Who's there?
Chicken.
Chicken who?
Just Chicken out the doorbell!

Knock–knock.

Who's there?
Chess game.
Chess game who?
Chess game to say goodbye.

Knock–knock.

Who's there?
Chester.
Chester who?
Chester little kid!

Knock–knock.

Who's there?
Chester.
Chester who?
"Chester song at twilight . . ."

Knock–knock.

Who's there?
Chesterfield.
Chesterfield who?
Chesterfield my leg, so
I slapped him.

Knock–knock.

Who's there?
Chihuahua (pronounced Chi-wah-wah).
Chihuahua who?
Chihuahua buy a magazine subscription?

Knock–knock.

Who's there?
Cindy.
Cindy who?
Cindy movie, read the book.

Knock–knock.

Who's there?
Cinnamon.
Cinnamon who?
Cinnamon-ster–
shut the door!

Knock–knock.

Who's there?
Clancy.
Clancy who?
Clancy where I'm going.

Knock–knock.

Who's there?
Colin.
Colin who?
Colin the doctor!
You make me sick.

Knock-knock.

Who's there?
Colleen.
Colleen who?
Colleen all cars!

Knock–knock.

Who's there?
Cologne.
Cologne who?
Cologne Ranger!

Knock–knock.

Who's there?
Collie.
Collie who?
Collie a taxi. I'm
leaving.

Knock–knock.

Who's there?
Coma.
Coma who?
Coma your hair.

Knock–knock.

Who's there?
Comma.
Comma who?
"Comma up and
see me sometime."

Knock–knock.

Who's there?
Concha.
Concha who?
Concha hear me knocking?

Knock–knock.

Who's there?
Conan.
Conan who?
Conan the cob.

Knock–knock.

Who's there?
Conscience stricken.
Conscience stricken who?
Don't conscience stricken
before they hatch.

Knock–knock.

Who's there?
Costanza.
Costanza who?
Costanza out here in the rain.
Open up!

Knock–knock.

Who's there?
Cows.
Cows who?
No, cows moo.

Knock–knock.

Who's there?
Cosmo.
Cosmo who?
You Cosmo trouble than
anybody I know.

Knock–knock.

Who's there?
Crassus.
Crassus who?
Crassus always greener on
the other side!

Knock–knock.

Who's there?
Crate.
Crate who?
Crate to be here.

Knock–knock.

Who's there?
Crepes.
Crepes who?
Crepes of Wrath.

Knock–knock.

Who's there?
Crimea
Crimea who?
"Crimea River."

Knock–knock.

Who's there?
Culligan.
Culligan who?
I'll Culligan when you have
something intelligent to say.

Knock–knock.

Who's there?
Cotton.
Cotton who?
Cotton off to a bad start!

Knock–knock.

Who's there?
Combat.
Combat who?
Combat tomorrow!

Knock–knock.

Who's there?
Culver.
Culver who?
Culver me up, I'm freezing.

Knock–knock.

Who's there?
Cy.
Cy who?
Cy knew it was you, I wouldn't have bothered knocking.

Knock–knock.

Who's there?
Cybil.
Cybil who?
Cybil War.

Knock–knock.

Who's there?
Cypress.
Cypress who?
Cypress your suit.

Knock–knock.

Who's there?
Czar.
Czar who?
Czar she blows!

Knock–knock.

Who's there?
Czar.
Czar who?
Czar-y about that!

Knock–knock.

Who's there?
Apollo.
Apollo who?
Apollo G. Accepted!

Knock–knock.

Who's there?
Czar.
Czar who?
Czar a doctor in
the house?

Knock–knock.

Who's there?
Dakar.
Dakar who?
Dakar has a flat tire!

Knock–knock.

Who's there?
Dakota.
Dakota who?
Dakota fits fine, the pants
are too long.

Knock–knock.

Who's there?
Dakota.
Dakota who?
Dakota many colors.

Knock–knock.

Who's there?
Damascus.
Damascus who?
Damascus slipping off da face.

Knock–knock.

Who's there?
Dandelion.
　Dandelion who?
Dandelion around out here,
but open the door anyway.

Knock–knock.

　Who's there?
Danielle.
　Danielle who?
Danielle at me, I heard you
the first time.

Knock–knock.

Who's there?
Dancer.
　Dancer who?
"Dancer, my friend, is blowing
in the wind . . ."

Knock–knock.

　Who's there?
Darby.
　Darby who?
Darby a lot of reasons why
I knocked.

Knock–knock.

Who's there?
Darby.
　Darby who?
Darby stung me.

Knock–knock.

Who's there?
Darren.
Darren who?
Darren you to
open the door!

Knock–knock.

Who's there?
Darth Vader.
Darth Vader who?
Darth Vader cookie crumbles.

Knock–knock.

Who's there?
Darwin.
Darwin who?
Darwin young man on the
flying trapeze.

Knock–knock.

Who's there?
Darwin.
Darwin who?
I'll be Darwin (there when)
you open the door.

Knock–knock.

Who's there?
Daryl.
Daryl who?
"Daryl never ever
be another you . . ."

Knock–knock.

Who's there?
Data.

Data who?
Data new hairdo or
did you just walk
through a car wash?

Knock–knock.

Who's there?
Datsun.

Datsun who?
Datsun old joke.

Knock–knock.

Who's there?
Daughter.

Daughter who?
Daughter-door salesman!

Knock–knock.

Who's there?
Dawn.

Dawn who?
Dawn bite off more than
you can chew.

Knock–knock.

Who's there?
Dawn.
Dawn who?
Dawn do anything
I wouldn't do.

Knock–knock.

Who's there?
Deanna.
Deanna who?
"Till Deanna time . . ."

Knock–knock.

Who's there?
Deanne.
Deanne who?
I'm Deanne-sir to
your prayers!

Knock–knock.

Who's there?
Debt.
Debt who?
Debt men tell no tales.

Knock–knock.

Who's there?
Dee Wallace.
Dee Wallace who?
"Dee Wallace came tumbling
down!"

Knock–knock.

Who's there?
Dee.
Dee who?
Dee joke's on me.

Knock–knock.

Who's there?
Defense.
Defense who?
Defense keeps the dog in.

Knock–knock.

Who's there?
Deluxe.
Deluxe who?
Deluxe Ness Monster.

Knock–knock.

Who's there?
Demand.
Demand who?
Demand from U.N.C.L.E.

Knock–knock.

Who's there?
Demure.
Demure who?
Demure the merrier.

Knock–knock.

Who's there?
Demure.
Demure who?
Demure you get, Demure you want.

Knock–knock.

Who's there?
Dennis.
Dennis who?
Dennis anyone?

Knock–knock.

Who's there?
Dennis.
Dennis who?
Dennis this rain going to stop?

Knock–knock.

Who's there?
Dennison.
Dennison who?
Dennison nice thing to say!

Knock–knock.

Who's there?
Dennis.
    Dennis who?
Dennis says I've got a cavity.

Knock–knock.

Who's there?
Denver.
    Denver who?
Denver in the world are we?

Knock–knock.

Who's there?
Denver.
    Denver who?
Denver the good
old days.

Knock–knock.

Who's there?
Depend.
    Depend who?
Depend is mightier than
the sword.

Knock–knock.

Who's there?
Derby.
Derby who?
Derby ghosts in that haunted house.

Knock–knock.

Who's there?
Desi.
Desi who?
Desi good reason why you think the world is against you—it is.

Knock–knock.

Who's there?
Derision.
Derision who?
Derision room for both of us in this town.

Knock–knock.

Who's there?
Deuce.
Deuce who?
Deuce something about your dog. He just bit me!

Knock–knock.

Who's there?
Dexter.
Dexter who?
"Dexter halls with
boughs of holly . . ."

Knock–knock.

Who's there?
D-1.
D-1 who?
I'm D-1 to watch.

Knock–knock.

Who's there?
Diane Kilburn.
Diane Kilburn who?
"Diane Kilburn's (the ankle
bone's) connected to the foot
bone . . ."

Knock–knock.

Who's there?
Diego.
Diego who?
Diego all over your face —
what a sloppy eater!

Knock–knock.

Who's there?
Diesel.
Diesel who?
Diesel be your last chance.

Knock–knock.

Who's there?
Diesel.
Diesel who?
"Diesel man, he played one, he played nick-nack on a drum . . ."

Knock–knock.

Who's there?
Dina.
Dina who?
Dina at eight.

Knock–knock.

Who's there?
Dion.
Dion who?
Dion of thirst—can I have a glass of water?

Knock–knock.

Who's there?
Dinosaur.
Dinosaur who?
Dinosaur at you—you burnt the toast.

Knock–knock.

Who's there?
Disease.
  Disease who?
Disease a disaster!

Knock–knock.

  Who's there?
Dishes.
  Dishes who?
Dishes the police—open
the door!

Knock–knock.

Who's there?
Dishwasher.
  Dishwasher who?
Dishwasher last chance.

Knock–knock.

  Who's there?
Divide.
  Divide who?
Divide world of sports.

Knock–knock.

Who's there?
Dizzy.
  Dizzy who?
Dizzy undertaker
know you're up?

Knock–knock.

Who's there?
Doberman pinscher.
Doberman pinscher who?
Doberman pinscher and she slugged him.

Knock–knock.

Who's there?
Dobie.
Dobie who?
Dobie cruel to animals.

Knock–knock.

Who's there?
Dodson.
Dodson who?
Dodson old knock-knock joke.

Knock–knock.

Who's there?
Dog Catcher.
Dog Catcher who?
Dog Catcher (don't count your) chickens before they hatch!

CHEEP CHEEP!

Knock–knock.

Who's there?
Dole.
Dole who?
Dole truth and nothing
but the truth.

Knock–knock.

Who's there?
Domino.
Domino who?
"Domino thing if you don't
have that swing . . ."

Knock–knock.

Who's there?
Don and Greta.
Don and Greta who?
Don and Greta round much
any more.

Knock–knock.

Who's there?
Don Blaine.
Don Blaine who?
Don Blaine (don't blame) me!

Knock–knock.

Who's there?
Don.
Don who?
Don mess around—
just open the door.

Knock–knock.

Who's there?
Don.
 Don who?
Don want to tell you
my name.

Knock–knock.

Who's there?
Dona Lewis.
 Dona Lewis who?
Dona Lewis (don't lose)
your temper!

Knock–knock.

Who's there?
Don Boris Witty.
 Don Boris Witty who?
Don Boris Witty details!

Knock–knock.

Who's there?
Don Juan.
 Don Juan who?
Don Juan to go out today?

Knock–knock.

Who's there?
Don Marcus.
 Don Marcus who?
Don Marcus absent, we're
right here!

Knock–knock.

Who's there?
Donahue.
Donahue who?
Donahue hide from
me, you rat.

Knock–knock.

Who's there?
Donald.
Donald who?
Donald (don't hold)
your breath!

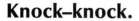

Knock–knock.

Who's there?
Donatello.
Donatello who?
Donatello anybody,
but I'm a werewolf.

Knock–knock.

Who's there?
Donat.
Donat who?
Donat be so smart.
Remember, you can
always be replaced
by a human being.

Knock–knock.

Who's there?
Donovan.
Donovan who?
Donovan think about it.

Knock–knock.

Who's there?
Donna.
Donna who?
"Way Donna-pon the
Swanee River . . ."

Knock–knock.

Who's there?
Donovan.
Donovan who?
Donovan to hear another
word out of you.

Knock–knock.

Who's there?
Dora Belle.
Dora Belle who?
Dora Belle is broken.
So I knocked.

Knock–knock.

Who's there?
Doris.
Doris who?
Doris no fool like an old fool!

Knock–knock.

Who's there?
Doughnut.
   Doughnut who?
Doughnut be afraid—it's only
me!

Knock–knock.

Who's there?
Doughnut.
   Doughnut who?
Doughnut thing till you
hear from me.

Knock–knock.

Who's there?
Dozer.
   Dozer who?
Dozer the breaks.

Knock–knock.

Who's there?
Dragon.
   Dragon who?
Dragon my name
through the mud?

Knock–knock.

Who's there?
Dragon.
Dragon who?
Quit Dragon
your tail!

Knock–knock.

Who's there?
Dresden.
Dresden who?
Dresden rags again?

Knock–knock.

Who's there?
Duane.
Duane who?
Duane the bathtub, rubber
ducky drowning.

Knock–knock.

Who's there?
Duet.
Duet who?
Duet right or don't
do it at all.

Knock–knock.

Who's there?
Druscilla.
Druscilla who?
Druscilla (drew a silly) picture of the teacher.

Knock–knock.

Who's there?
Mamie.
Mamie who?
She Mamie erase it.

Knock–knock.

Who's there?
Dudes.
Dudes who?
Dudes and don'ts.

Knock–knock.

Who's there?
Dunbar.
Dunbar who?
Dunbar the door—I'll only climb through the window.

Knock–knock.

Who's there?
Duncan.
Duncan who?
Duncan Donuts.

Knock–knock.

Who's there?
Dustin.
   Dustin who?
Dustin furniture with polish.

Knock–knock.

Who's there?
Dutch.
   Dutch who?
Dutch me and I'll scream.

Knock–knock.

Who's there?
Dwight.
   Dwight who?
Dwight as rain.

Knock–knock.

Who's there?
Dwayne.
   Dwayne who?
"Dwayne in Spain falls mainly
in the plain . . ."

Knock–knock.

Who's there?
Wayne.
   Wayne who?
"Wayne, Wayne go away,
come again another day!"

Knock–knock.

Who's there?
Eamon.
Eamon who?
Eamon the mood for love.

Knock–knock.

Who's there?
Easter.
Easter who?
Easter anybody home?

Knock–knock.

Who's there?
Eaton.
Eaton who?
Eaton out of the garbage again?

Knock–knock.

Who's there?
Eben.
Eben who?
Eben a good girl.

Knock–knock.

Who's there?
Ed Rather.
Ed Rather who?
Ed Rather be sailing!

Knock–knock.

Who's there?
Eddy.
Eddy who?
Eddy body got a tissue?
I've got a cold.

Knock–knock.

Who's there?
Edward B.
Edward B. who?
Edward B. nice if you
made like a bee and
buzzed off.

Knock–knock.

Who's there?
Efficient.
Efficient who?
Efficient my old pal!

Knock–knock.

Who's there?
Effie.
Effie who?
Effie-thing I have
is yours.

Knock–knock.

Who's there?
Effie.
Effie who?
"Effie Thing's Coming Up
Roses."

Knock–knock.

Who's there?
Eggs.
Eggs who?
Eggs marks the spot.

Knock–knock.

Who's there?
Egos.
Egos who?
Egos wherever he wants to.

Knock–knock.

Who's there?
Egypt.
Egypt who?
Egypt you when he sold you
that busted doorbell.

Knock–knock.

Who's there?
Eiffel Tower.
Eiffel Tower who?
Eiffel (I feel) Towerable!

Knock–knock.

Who's there?
Elaine.
Elaine who?
Elaine down to take a nap.

Knock–knock.

Who's there?
Ma Belle.
Ma Belle who?
Ma Belle E. aches.

Knock–knock.

Who's there?
Cara Mia.
Cara Mia who?
Cara Mia to the doctor!

Knock–knock.

Who's there?
Eileen Dunn.
Eileen Dunn who?
Eileen Dunn the bell
and it broke.

Knock–knock.

Who's there?
Eiffel.
Eiffel who?
Eiffel down and hurt
my knee.

Knock–knock.

Who's there?
Antony.
Antony who?
Antony still hurts.

Knock–knock.

Who's there?
Eisenhower.
Eisenhower who?
Eisenhower late—sorry!

Knock–knock.

Who's there?
Elia.
Elia who?
Elia wake at night
thinking about you.

Knock–knock.

Who's there?
Elise.
Elise who?
Elise signed by a tenant.

Knock–knock.

Who's there?
Eliza.
Eliza who?
Eliza lot, so watch
your step.

Knock–knock.

Who's there?
Ella Mann.
Ella Mann who?
Ella Mann-tary, my
dear Watson.

Knock–knock.

Who's there?
Ella.
Ella who?
Ella-vator.
Doesn't that give
you a lift?

Knock–knock.

Who's there?
Ella Vance.
Ella Vance who?
Ella Vance never forget.

Knock–knock.

Who's there?
Elke.
Elke who?
"Elke seltzer . . .
Plop, plop,
fizz, fizz . . ."

Knock–knock.

Who's there?
Ellen.
Ellen who?
Ellen-eed is love.

Knock–knock.

Who's there?
Emanuel.
Emanuel who?
Emanuel see turn into
a werewolf when the
moon is full.

Knock–knock.

Who's there?
Emerson.
Emerson who?
Emerson of a gun!

Knock–knock.

Who's there?
Emissary.
Emissary who?
Emissary I made you cry.

Knock–knock.

Who's there?
Emma Lou King.
Emma Lou King who?
Emma Lou King into
my crystal ball . . .

Knock–knock.

Who's there?
Emma.
Emma who?
Emma Nemms!

Knock–knock.

Who's there?
Encino.
Encino who?
Hear no evil, speak
no evil, Encino evil!

Knock–knock.

Who's there?
Enid Sue.
Enid Sue who?
Enid Sue like a hole
in the head!

Knock–knock.

Who's there?
Erie.
Erie who?
Erie is, right on time.

Knock–knock.

Who's there?
Errol.
Errol who?
Errol be a hot time in
the old town tonight!

Knock–knock.

Who's there?
Eskimo.
Eskimo who?
Eskimo questions—
I'll tell you no lies.

Knock–knock.

Who's there?
Eschew.
Eschew who?
Eschew goes on your foot.

Knock–knock.

Who's there?
Estelle.
   Estelle who?
Estelle am waiting
for you to open
this door!

Knock–knock.

Who's there?
Etch.
   Etch who?
Bless you.

Knock–knock.

Who's there?
Ethan.
   Ethan who?
Ethan everything in sight.

Knock–knock.

Who's there?
Ethan.
   Ethan who?
Ethan this the pits?

Knock–knock.

Who's there?
Etta.
   Etta who?
Etta Boy!

Knock–knock.

Who's there?
Ether.
Ether who?
Ether Bunny.

Knock–knock.

Who's there?
Cargo.
Cargo who?
Cargo "beep-beep" and
run over Ether Bunny.

Knock–knock.

Who's there?
Stella.
Stella who?
Stella 'nother Ether Bunny.

Knock–knock.

Who's there?
Consumption.
Consumption who?
Consumption be done about
all these Ether Bunnies?

Knock–knock.

Who's there?
Etta May Whit.
Etta May Whit who?
Etta May Whit- (At my wits')
send!

Knock–knock.

Who's there?
Eubie.
Eubie who?
Eubie-lieve in law and
order—if you lay down
the law and give the order.

Knock–knock.

Who's there?
Eudora Belle.
Eudora Belle who?
Eudora Belle thing, you!

Knock–knock.

Who's there?
Eubie.
Eubie who?
"Eubie long to me . . ."

Knock–knock.

Who's there?
Eugenes.
Eugenes who?
Eugenes need washing.

Knock–knock.

Who's there?
Eudora.
Eudora who?
Eudora is stuck!

Knock–knock.

Who's there?
Eureka.

Eureka who?
Eureka perfume! Who
sold it to you—a skunk?

Knock–knock.

Who's there?
Europa.

Europa who?
Europa steer and I'll watch.

Knock–knock.

Who's there?
European.

European who?
European in the
neck.

Knock–knock.

Who's there?
Europe.

Europe who?
Europe (you're up)
to no good!

Knock–knock.

Who's there?
Evan.

Evan who?
Evan Lee coffee!

Knock–knock.

Who's there?
Evan.

Evan who?
Evan seen anything like you
since the Rocky Horror Show.

Knock–knock.

Who's there?
Ewell.
Ewell who?
Ewell catch more flies with
honey than with vinegar!

Knock–knock.

Who's there?
Ewer.
Ewer who?
Ewer getting sleepy.

Knock–knock.

Who's there?
Eye Sore.
Eye Sore who?
Eye Sore them coming!

Knock–knock.

Who's there?
Eyelet.
Eyelet who?
Eyelet you in.

Knock–knock.

Who's there?
Eyes.
Eyes who?
Eyes got another
knock-knock joke.

Knock–knock.

Who's there?
Nose.
Nose who?
I nose another
knock-knock joke.

Knock–knock.

Who's there?
Ears.
Ears who?
Ears another
knock-knock joke.

Knock–knock.

Who's there?
Chin.
Chin who?
Chin up—I'm not going to tell
any more knock-knock jokes.

Knock–knock.

Who's there?
Falsetto.
Falsetto who?
Falsetto teeth.

Knock–knock.

Who's there?
Fallacy.
Fallacy who?
I Fallacy (fail to see)
what's so funny!

Knock–knock.

Who's there?
F-2.
F-2 who?
Do I F-2 tell you?

Knock–knock.

Who's there?
Fanny.
Fanny who?
Fanny body calls,
I'm out.

Knock–knock.

Who's there?
Fanny.
Fanny who?
Fanny you should ask!

Knock–knock.

Who's there?
Far Side.
Far Side who?
As Far Side (far as I) know,
it's still me!

Knock–knock.

Who's there?
Faraday.
Faraday who?
Faraday last time,
open up!

Knock–knock.

Who's there?
Farrah.
Farrah who?
Farrah 'n wide.

Knock–knock.

Who's there?
Farrah.
Farrah who?
Farrah out, man.

Knock–knock.

Who's there?
Farris.
Farris who?
"Mirror, mirror on the wall. Who's the Farris one of all?"

Knock–knock.

Who's there?
Father.
Father who?
The Father the better!

Knock–knock.

Who's there?
Fatso Kay.
Fatso Kay who?
Fatso Kay with you, Fatso Kay with me!

Knock–knock.

Who's there?
Fedora.
Fedora who?
Fedora shut, does that mean I can't come in?

Knock–knock.

Who's there?
Felix.
Felix who?
Felix-cited all over.

Knock–knock.

Who's there?
Fender.
Fender who?
Fender moon comes over the mountain.

Knock–knock.

Who's there?
Ferdie.
Ferdie who?
Ferdie last time, open the door!

Knock–knock.

Who's there?
Ferdinand.
Ferdinand who?
Ferdinand is worth two in the bush.

Knock–knock.

Who's there?
Ferrara.
Ferrara who?
"Long ago and Ferrara-way . . ."

Knock–knock.

Who's there?
Ferris.
Ferris who?
Ferris I'm concerned, we're through.

Knock–knock.

Who's there?
Fess.
Fess who?
Fess Aid Squad.

Knock–knock.

Who's there?
Fiddlesticks.
Fiddlesticks who?
Fiddlesticks (feet'll stick) out
if the blanket's too short.

Knock–knock.

Who's there?
Fidel.
Fidel who?
Fidel you a secret, will
you keep it to yourself?

Knock–knock.

Who's there?
Fido.
Fido who?
Fido away, what
will you give me?

Knock–knock.

Who's there?
Fiendish.
   Fiendish who?
Fiendish your dinner!

Knock–knock.

Who's there?
Fission.
   Fission who?
Fission for compliments!

Knock–knock.

   Who's there?
Fiona.
(Pronounced Fee-oh-na)
   Fiona who?
Fiona had something better
to do, do you think we'd
hang around here?

Knock–knock.

   Who's there?
Fitzhugh.
   Fitzhugh who?
If the shoe Fitzhugh wear it!

Knock–knock.

Who's there?
Fletcher.
   Fletcher who?
Fletcher self go!

Knock–knock.

   Who's there?
Flaherty.
   Flaherty who?
Flaherty will get you nowhere!

Knock–knock.

Who's there?
Flea.
Flea who?
"Flea, fie, foh, fum."

Knock–knock.

Who's there?
Florist.
Florist who?
Florist the opposite of ceiling.

Knock–knock.

Who's there?
Florist.
Florist who?
You can't see the
Florist for the trees!

Knock–knock.

Who's there?
Flossie.
Flossie who?
Flossie your teeth.

Knock–knock.

Who's there?
Fonzi.
Fonzi who?
Fonzi meeting you here!

Knock–knock.

Who's there?
Ford.
Ford who?
Ford-y thieves.

Knock–knock.

Who's there?
Foreign.
Foreign who?
"Foreign twenty blackbirds
baked in a pie . . ."

Knock–knock.

Who's there?
Forest.
Forest who?
Forest the eye can see.

Knock–knock.

Who's there?
Formosa.
Formosa who?
Formosa my life, I've
been waiting for you
to open the door!

Knock–knock.

Who's there?
Formosa.
Formosa who?
Formosa the day I've had my
foot stuck in this door.

Knock–knock.

Who's there?
Fortification.
Fortification who?
Fortification I go to the seashore.

Knock–knock.

Who's there?
Forty.
Forty who?
Forty last time, open up!

Knock–knock.

Who's there?
Francine.
Francine who?
Francine it all.

Knock–knock.

Who's there?
Frank.
Frank who?
Frank N. Stein. Aaggh!

Knock–knock.

Who's there?
Frank Lee.
Frank Lee who?
Frank Lee, it's none of your
business.

Knock–knock.

Who's there?
Frank's eye.
Frank's eye who?
Frank's eye needed that.

Knock–knock.

Who's there?
Franz.
Franz who?
"Franz, Romans, countrymen . . ."

Knock–knock.

Who's there?
Franz.
Franz who?
Franz forever!

Knock–knock.

Who's there?
Fred.
Fred who?
Fred I'll have to tell
you another joke.

Knock–knock.

Who's there?
Freddie.
Freddie who?
Freddie or not, here
I come.

Knock–knock.

Who's there?
Freedom.
Freedom who?
Never mind—let
freedom ring.

Knock–knock.

Who's there?
Free Stew.
Free Stew who?
The Free Stew-ges
(The Three Stooges).

Knock–knock.

Who's there?
Freighter.
Freighter who?
Freighter open the door?

Knock–knock.

Who's there?
Freeze.
Freeze who?
"Freeze a jolly good fellow . . ."

Knock–knock.

Who's there?
Freud.
Freud who?
A-Freud you were going to ask that.

Knock–knock.

Who's there?
Fresno.
Fresno who?
"Rudolf the Fresno reindeer . . ."

Knock–knock.

Who's there?
Frieda.
Frieda who?
Who's a Frieda the big bad wolf?

Knock–knock.

Who's there?
Fritz.
Fritz who?
"Fritz a Wonderful Life."

Knock–knock.

Who's there?
Fu Manchu.
Fu Manchu who?
Fu Manchu bubble gum the way you do.

Knock–knock.

Who's there?
GM.
    GM who?
GM I rattling your cage?

Knock–knock.

Who's there?
Galahad.
    Galahad who?
I knew a Galahad
two left feet!

Knock–knock.

Who's there?
Gallo.
    Gallo who?
Gallo your dreams.

Knock–knock.

Who's there?
Garcia.
    Garcia who?
Garcia (go see) the
principal.

Knock–knock.

Who's there?
Garter.
    Garter who?
Garter date with an angel.

Knock–knock.

Who's there?
Garter.
Garter who?
Garter go now!

Knock–knock.

Who's there?
Gary.
Gary who?
Gary the package for me.

Knock–knock.

Who's there?
Gas.
Gas who?
"Gas Who's Coming to Dinner."

Knock–knock.

Who's there?
Gauguin.
Gauguin who?
Gauguin, it's your turn!

Knock–knock.

Who's there?
Gavin.
Gavin who?
Gavin you one more chance
to open the door!

Knock–knock.

Who's there?
Dustin.
Dustin who?
Dustin off the battering ram!

Knock–knock.

Who's there?
Germaine.
Germaine who?
Germaine (you're mean) to act
this way!

Knock–knock.

Who's there?
Ghana.
Ghana who?
Not Ghana take this anymore.

Knock–knock.

Who's there?
G.I.
G.I. who?
G.I. don't know.

Knock–knock.

Who's there?
Gideon.
Gideon who?
Gideon your horse and let's go!

Knock–knock.

Who's there?
Gillette.
Gillette who?
If Gillette me in, I won't
knock anymore.

Knock–knock.

Who's there?
Gladwin.
Gladwin who?
Gladwin you leave town.

Knock–knock.

Who's there?
Gladys.
Gladys who?
Gladys see you.

Knock–knock.

Who's there?
Giovanni.
Giovanni who?
Giovanni come out and play?

Knock–knock.

Who's there?
Festival.
Festival who?
Festival I have to do my homework.

Knock–knock.

Who's there?
Gibbon.
Gibbon who?
Are you Gibbon me trouble?

Knock–knock.

Who's there?
Gil Diaz.
Gil Diaz who?
Gil Diaz (guilty as) charged!

Knock–knock.

Who's there?
Giuseppe.
Giuseppe who?
Giuseppe (just stepped) in
something on your doorstep.

Knock–knock.

Who's there?
Houdini.
Houdini who?
Houdini that thing on
your doorstep?

Knock–knock.

Who's there?
Glove.
Glove who?
"Glove is a Many-Splendored
Thing."

Knock–knock.

Who's there?
G-Man.
G-Man who?
G-Man-y Crickets!

Knock–knock.

Who's there?
Goat.
Goat who?
Goat to your room!

Knock–knock.

Who's there?
Goatee.
　　Goatee who?
Goatee off—the other golfers
are waiting.

Knock–knock.

Who's there?
Goddard.
　　Goddard who?
You Goddard be kidding!

Knock–knock.

Who's there?
Goddess.
　　Goddess who?
Goddess stop meeting
like this.

Knock–knock.

Who's there?
Goody.
　　Goody who?
"Goody-vening!" says
Count Dracula.

Knock–knock.

Who's there?
Venom.
　　Venom who?
Venom I going to get inside?

Knock–knock.

Who's there?
Goliath.
Goliath who?
Goliath down. You're
sick in the head.

Knock–knock.

Who's there?
Goosie.
Goosie who?
Goosie who's at the door.

Knock–knock.

Who's there?
Gopher.
Gopher who?
Gopher (go for) broke.

Knock–knock.

Who's there?
Gordie.
Gordie who?
Gordie-rectly to jail.
Do not pass Go.
Do not collect $200.

Knock–knock.

Who's there?
Gorilla.
Gorilla who?
Gorilla cheese sandwich.

Knock–knock.

Who's there?
Gouda.
Gouda who?
Gouda see you again.

Knock–knock.

Who's there?
Grammar.
Grammar who?
Grammar crackers. Pretty crummy, huh?

Knock–knock.

Who's there?
Gray Z.
Gray Z. who?
Gray Z. mixed-up kid!

Knock–knock.

Who's there?
Greta.
Greta who?
You Greta my nerves.

Knock–knock.

Who's there?
Gretel.

Gretel who?
"Gretel-long little dogie . . ."

Knock–knock.

Who's there?
Gruesome.

Gruesome who?
Gruesome tomatoes in
my garden.

Knock–knock.

Who's there?
Guava.

Guava who?
Guava good time!

Knock–knock.

Who's there?
Guinevere.

Guinevere who?
Guinevere going to
get together?

Knock–knock.

Who's there?
Gucci.
   Gucci who?
Gucci-Gucci-Goo!

Knock–knock.

Who's there?
Guinness.
   Guinness who?
Guinness a break!

Knock–knock.

Who's there?
Gunboat.
   Gunboat who?
You're Gunboat not
forgotten.

Knock–knock.

Who's there?
Gummy.
   Gummy who?
Gummy five!

Knock–knock.

Who's there?
Gus.
    Gus who?
That's what *you're* supposed
to do.

Knock–knock.

Who's there?
Gunnar.
    Gunnar who?
Gunnar huff and puff
and blow your house in.

Knock–knock.

Who's there?
Guthrie.
    Guthrie who?
Guthrie blind mice.

Knock–knock.

Who's there?
Gwen N.
    Gwen N. who?
Gwen N. bear it!

Knock–knock.

Who's there?
Gwen.
    Gwen who?
Gwen will I see you again?

Knock–knock.

Who's there?
Habit.
    Habit who?
Habit your own way!

Knock–knock.

Who's there?
Hackett.
    Hackett who?
I can't Hackett–
I'm going home.

Knock–knock.

Who's there?
Haiku.
    Haiku who?
"Haiku-d have danced
all night . . ."

Knock–knock.

Who's there?
Hair combs.
    Hair combs who?
Hair combs the bride.

Knock–knock.

Who's there?
Hair combs.
Hair combs who?
Hair combs the judge!

Knock–knock.

Who's there?
Half.
Half who?
Half I got a girl for you.

Knock–knock.

Who's there?
Halibut.
Halibut who?
Halibut lending me
five dollars?

Knock–knock.

Who's there?
Hall.
Hall who?
"Hall the king's horses and
hall the king's men."

Knock–knock.

Who's there?
Hallow.
Hallow who?
Hallow down there.

Knock–knock.

Who's there?
Hallways.

Hallways who?
Hallways knew you'd
never amount to much.

Customer: **Knock–knock.**
Waiter: Who's there?
Customer: Hammond.
Waiter: Hammond who?
Customer: Hammond eggs,
              please.

Knock–knock.

Who's there?
Hannah.

Hannah who?
"Hannah partridge
in a pear tree . . ."

Knock–knock.

Who's there?
Hannibal.

Hannibal who?
Hannibal in a china shop.

Knock–knock.

Who's there?
Hanover.

Hanover who?
Hanover your money.

Knock–knock.

Who's there?
Hans.
Hans who?
Hans up! I'm a burglar.

Knock–knock.

Who's there?
Jimmy.
Jimmy who?
Jimmy your money—or else!

Knock–knock.

Who's there?
Bruce.
Bruce who?
Careful—I Bruce easily.

Knock–knock.

Who's there?
Hans.
Hans who?
Hans off my computer.

Knock–knock.

Who's there?
Hardy.
   Hardy who?
Hardy, har, har!

Knock–knock.

Who's there?
Harley.
   Harley who?
Harley ever see you around anymore.

Knock–knock.

Who's there?
Harmon.
   Harmon who?
Harmon your side.

Knock–knock.

Who's there?
Harmony.
   Harmony who?
Harmony times do I have to knock at this door?

Knock–knock.

Who's there?
Harpy.
   Harpy who?
Harpy to see you again.

Knock–knock.

Who's there?
Harold.
Harold who?
Harold are you?

Knock–knock.

Who's there?
Harris.
Harris who?
"Harris looking at you, kid."

Knock–knock.

Who's there?
Harris.
Harris who?
Harris the world treating you?

Knock–knock.

Who's there?
Harry.
Harry who?
Harry up, I'm starving.

Knock–knock.

Who's there?
Harrison.
    Harrison who?
Harrison idea—you tell the
next joke!

Knock–knock.

Who's there?
Hartley.
    Hartley who?
This is Hartley the time to
be telling knock-knock jokes!

Knock–knock.

Who's there?
Harv and Hugh.
    Harv and Hugh who?
Harv and Hugh (haven't you)
got a minute?

Knock–knock.

Who's there?
Harvard.
    Harvard who?
Harvard you like a punch
in the nose?

Knock–knock.

Who's there?
Harvey.
    Harvey who?
Harvey going to stop meeting
like this?

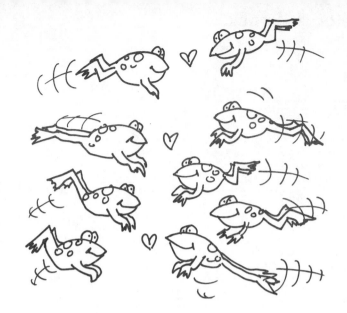

Knock–knock.

Who's there?
Harvey.
Harvey who?
Harvey going to play this
game forever?

Knock–knock.

Who's there?
Harvey Gotti.
Harvey Gotti who?
Harvey Gotti wait here all
night?

Knock–knock.

Who's there?
Hattie.
Hattie who?
Hattie do, you all!

Knock–knock.

Who's there?
Hawaii.
Hawaii who?
Hawaii doing?

Knock–knock.

Who's there?
Healy.
Healy who?
Healy my pain . . .

Knock–knock.

Who's there?
Heath.
Heath who?
"For Heath a jolly
good fellow . . ."

Knock–knock.

Who's there?
Heaven.
Heaven who?
Heaven you heard enough
knock-knock jokes?

Knock–knock.

Who's there?
Heaven.
Heaven who?
Heaven seen you
for a long time.

Knock–knock.

Who's there?
Hector.
Hector who?
"Hector halls with boughs
of holly."

Knock–knock.

Who's there?
Hedda.

Hedda who?
Hedda feeling you wouldn't
open the door.

Knock–knock.

Who's there?
Hedda.

Hedda who?
Hedda I win, tails
you lose!

Knock–knock.

Who's there?
Hedda.

Hedda who?
Hedda off at the pass.

Knock–knock.

Who's there?
Heidi.

Heidi who?
Heidi-clare war on you!

Knock–knock.

Who's there?
Heidi.
Heidi who?
Heidi go seek.

Knock–knock.

Who's there?
Heifer.
Heifer who?
Heifer (half a) cow
is better than none.

Knock–knock.

Who's there?
Hello Etta.
Hello Etta who?
"Hello Etta, gentille Alouetta . . ."

Knock–knock.

Who's there?
Henny.
Henny who?
Henny Penny. The sky
is falling down!

Knock–knock.

Who's there?
Izzy.
Izzy who?
Izzy end of the world!

Knock–knock.

Who's there?
Henrietta.
Henrietta who?
Henrietta big dinner and
got sick.

Knock–knock.

Who's there?
Romeo and Juliet.
Romeo and Juliet who?
Romeo and Juliet the same
thing—and died.

HEE
HEE

Knock–knock.

Who's there?
Hester.
Hester who?
Hester any food left?

Knock–knock.

Who's there?
Pasadena.
Pasadena who?
Pasadena under the door—I'm
starved.

Knock–knock.

Who's there?
Hertz.
Hertz who?
Hertz me more than it hurts you.

Knock–knock.

Who's there?
Hewlett.
Hewlett who?
Hewlett you out of your cage?

Knock–knock.

Who's there?
Heywood, Hugh and Harry.
Heywood, Hugh and Harry
who?
Heywood, Hugh Harry and
open the door!

Knock–knock.

Who's there?
Hiawatha.
Hiawatha who?
Hiawatha very bad today.

Knock–knock.

Who's there?
Highway cop.
Highway cop who?
Highway cop at seven every morning.

Knock–knock.

Who's there?
Highway cop.
Highway cop who?
Highway cop screaming—
thinking of you.

Knock–knock.

Who's there?
Hippie.
Hippie who?
Hippie birthday to you.

Knock–knock.

Who's there?
Hiram.
Hiram who?
Hiram fine, how are you?

Knock–knock.

Who's there?
Hiram.
Hiram who?
Hiram glad you asked!

Knock–knock.

Who's there?
Hobbit.
Hobbit who?
Hobbit letting me in?

Knock–knock.

Who's there?
Holden.
Holden who?
Holden up everything
on account of you.

Knock–knock.

Who's there?
Hollis.
Hollis who?
Come back, Hollis
(all is) forgiven!

Knock–knock.

Who's there?
Holmes.
Holmes who?
Holmes sweet home.

Knock–knock.

Who's there?
Hominy.
Hominy who?
Hominy rocks did they
have to turn up before
you crawled out?

Knock–knock.

Who's there?
Honda.
Honda who?
"Home, home Honda range . . ."

Knock–knock.

Who's there?
Honda.
Honda who?
Honda road again!

Knock–knock.

Who's there?
Honeydew.
Honeydew who?
Honeydew you think you're
ever going to open the door?

Knock–knock.

Who's there?
Honorless.
Honorless who?
Honorless you open this door,
I'll have to break it down!

Knock–knock.

Who's there?
Honor.
Honor who?
"Honor clear day you can see
forever."

Knock–knock.

Who's there?
Hoover.
Hoover who?
Hoover you expecting?

Knock–knock.

Who's there?
Horace.
Horace who?
Horace and buggy.

Knock–knock.

Who's there?
Horace.
Horace who?
Horace of a different color!

Knock–knock.

Who's there?
Horace.
Horace who?
Horace I to know you lived here?

Knock–knock.

Who's there?
House.
House who?
House it going?

Knock–knock.

Who's there?
Howard.
Howard who?
Howard I know?

Knock–knock.

Who's there?
Hoodoo.
Hoodoo who?
Hoodoo you want it to be?

Knock–knock.

Who's there?
San Juan.
San Juan who?
San Juan (someone) else!

Knock–knock.

Who's there?
Howard.
Howard who?
Howard you like to crawl back
under your rock?

Knock–knock.

Who's there?
Howell.
Howell who?
Howell I get in if you don't
answer the door?

Knock–knock.

Who's there?
Hubie Maddern.
Hubie Maddern who?
Hubie Maddern a wet hen!

Knock–knock.

Who's there?
Hugh.
Hugh who?
Hugh who yourself.

Knock–knock.

Who's there?
Hugh Hefner.
Hugh Hefner who?
Hugh Hefner trouble with the
doorknob again?

Knock–knock.

Who's there?
Hugo N.
Hugo N. who?
Hugo N. Crazy—
and I'm goin' home.

Knock–knock.

Who's there?
Humus.
Humus who?
Humus be sick—that can't be your real face!

Tap–tap.

Who's there?
Hurd.
Hurd who?
Hurd my hand so I can't knock-knock.

Knock–knock.

Who's there?
Humphrey.
Humphrey who?
Humphrey ever blowing bubbles.

Knock–knock.

Who's there?
Hunger.
Hunger who?
Hunger wash out to dry.

Knock–knock.

Who's there?
Huron.
Huron who?
Huron time for once.

Knock–knock.

Who's there?
Huron.
Huron who?
Huron away from
home again?

Knock–knock.

Who's there?
Hutch.
Hutch who?
Gersundheit!

Knock–knock.

Who's there?
Hy.
Hy who?
Hy-oh, Silver!

Knock–knock.

Who's there?
Hyam Alda.
Hyam Alda who?
Hyam Alda washed up.

Knock–knock.

Who's there?
I.B. Long.
 I.B. Long who?
I.B. Long inside.
It's cold out here.

Knock–knock.

Who's there?
Ice water.
 Ice water who?
My ice water when I chop onions!

Knock–knock.

Who's there?
Ice water.
 Ice water who?
Ice water fly with my fly swatter.

Knock–knock.

Who's there?
Ice cream soda.
 Ice cream soda who?
Ice cream soda (I scream so the) whole
world will know what a nut you are.

Knock–knock.

Who's there?
Ichabod.
Ichabod who?
Ichabod (it's a bad)
night out. Can I
borrow your umbrella?

Knock–knock.

Who's there?
Icon.
Icon who?
Icon live without you!

Knock–knock.

Who's there?
Ida Clair.
Ida Clair who?
Ida Clair, you're the
most stubborn person!

Knock–knock.

Who's there?
Ida Klein.
Ida Klein who?
Ida Klein to answer
that question!

Knock–knock.

Who's there?
Ida.
   Ida who?
Ida know. Sorry.

Knock–knock.

Who's there?
Ida.
   Ida who?
Ida who potato.

Knock–knock.

Who's there?
Ida.
   Ida who?
Idaho—not Ida-who!
Can't you spell?

Knock–knock.

Who's there?
Igloo.
   Igloo who?
"Igloo knew Suzie like I know Suzie . . ."

Knock–knock.

Who's there?
Igor.
   Igor who?
Igor to see you again.

Knock–knock.

Who's there?
Imus.
Imus who?
Imus get in out of the rain.

Knock–knock.

Who's there?
Ina Claire.
Ina Claire who?
"Ina Claire day, you can see forever . . ."

Knock–knock.

Who's there?
India.
India who?
"India good old summertime . . ."

Knock–knock.

Who's there?
Indonesia.
Indonesia who?
I look at you and I get weak Indonesia.

Knock–knock.

Who's there?
Indochina.
Indochina who?
The bull Indochina shop.

Knock–knock.

Who's there?
Indy.
     Indy who?
Indy mood.

Knock–knock.

     Who's there?
Iodine.
     Iodine who?
Iodine (I'm a dyin') for a pizza!

Knock–knock.

Who's there?
Iona.
     Iona who?
"Iona have one life to
give for my country . . ."

Knock–knock.

     Who's there?
Iona.
     Iona who?
"Iona have eyes for you . . ."

Knock–knock.

Who's there?
I-one.
I-one who?
"I-one-der who's kissing her now . . ."

Knock–knock.

Who's there?
Ira.
Ira who?
Ira-turn with another knock-knock joke.

Knock–knock.

Who's there?
Iraq.
Iraq who?
Iraq my brain but couldn't get the answer.

Knock–knock.

Who's there?
Iraq and Iran.
Iraq and Iran who?
Iraq'd up the car and
Iran all the way over.

Knock–knock.

Who's there?
Iris.
   Iris who?
Iris you were here.

Knock–knock.

Who's there?
Irish.
   Irish who?
Irish upon a star.

Knock–knock.

Who's there?
Irish Stew.
   Irish Stew who?
Irish Stew would come out and play.

Knock–knock.

Who's there?
Irma.
   Irma who?
Irma going to sit right down
and write myself a letter.

Knock–knock.

Who's there?
Iron.
   Iron who?
Iron joy being a girl.

Knock–knock.

Who's there?
Isadore.
Isadore who?
Isadore stuck?

Knock–knock.

Who's there?
Isabelle.
Isabelle who?
Isabelle broken?

Knock–knock.

Who's there?
Isaiah.
Isaiah who?
Isaiah there, old chap, why
don't you open the door?

Knock–knock.

Who's there?
Israel.
Israel who?
Israel or fake?

Knock–knock.

Who's there?
Issue.
Issue who?
Issue ready to go?

Knock–knock.

Who's there?
Istanbul.
Istanbul who?
Istanbul fight over?

Knock–knock.

Who's there?
Isthmus.
Isthmus who?
Isthmus be the right place.

Knock–knock.

Who's there?
Itzhak.
Itzhak who?
"Itzhak small world after all."

Knock–knock.

Who's there?
Ivan.
Ivan who?
Ivan infectious disease.

Knock–knock.

Who's there?
Ivan.
Ivan who?
"Ivan working on the railroad . . ."

Knock–knock.

Who's there?
Ivan.
Ivan who?
Ivan, you lose.

Knock–knock.

Who's there?
Ivy Leaf.
Ivy Leaf who?
Ivy Leaf you alone.

Knock–knock.

Who's there?
Jack N.
Jack N. who?
Jack N. the Box.

Knock–knock.

Who's there?
Jackal.
Jackal who?
Jackal lantern.

Knock–knock.

Who's there?
Janet R.
Janet R. who?
Janet R. in a drum.

Knock–knock.

Who's there?
Java.
Java who?
Java lot to learn!

Knock–knock.

Who's there?
Jason.
Jason who?
"I'm always Jason rainbows..."

Knock–knock.

Who's there?
Jaws.
Jaws who?
Jaws till the well runs dry.

Knock–knock.

Who's there?
Jeff.
Jeff who?
Jeff Boy-R-Dee.

Knock–knock.

Who's there?
Jenny.
Jenny who?
Jenny a hearing aid? I've been knocking for five minutes.

Knock–knock.

Who's there?
Jenny.
Jenny who?
Jenny body home?

Knock–knock.

Who's there?
Jenny.
Jenny who?
Jenny'd any help opening the door?

Knock–knock.

Who's there?
Jericho.
Jericho who?
Jericho to Disneyland?

Knock–knock.

Who's there?
Jerome.
Jerome who?
Have it Jerome way!

Knock–knock.

Who's there?
Jess B.
Jess B. who?
Jess B. Cuzz!

Knock–knock.

Who's there?
Jess.
Jess who?
Jess in time.

Knock–knock.

Who's there?
Jess.
Jess who?
Jess knock it off!

Knock–knock.

Who's there?
Jess me.
Jess me who?
"Jess me and my shadow . . ."

Knock–knock.

Who's there?
Jess Horace.
Jess Horace who?
Jess Horace-n' around!

Knock–knock.

Who's there?
Jess.
Jess who?
Jess one of those things.

2001 Knock-Knocks & Tongue Twisters

Knock–knock.

Who's there?
Jessica.
Jessica who?
Jessica (you're sicker)
than I thought.

Knock–knock.

Who's there?
Jester.
Jester who?
Jester minute, pardner.

Knock–knock.

Who's there?
Jester.
Jester who?
Jester minute, I've got more
knock-knock jokes!

Knock–knock.

Who's there?
Jethro.
Jethro who?
Jethro (just throw) me
a few bones.

Knock–knock.

Who's there?
Jethro.
Jethro who?
Jethro the boat and
stop talking so much.

Knock–knock.

Who's there?
Jewel.
Jewel who?
Jewel (you'll) remember me
after you see my face.

Knock–knock.

Who's there?
Jewel.
Jewel who?
Jewel be sorry.

Knock–knock.

Who's there?
Jezebel.
Jezebel who?
Jezebel on the door,
but it won't ring.

Knock–knock.

Who's there?
Jimmy.
Jimmy who?
Jimmy liberty or Jimmy death.

Knock–knock.

Who's there?
Joe King.
Joe King who?
You must be Joe King!

Knock–knock.

Who's there?
Jock.
Jock who?
Jock-late milk shake.

Knock–knock.

Who's there?
Johann Sebastian Bach.
Johann Sebastian Bach who?
Johann Sebastian Bach in town!

Knock–knock.

Who's there?
John Q.
John Q. who?
John Q. very much.

Knock–knock.

Who's there?
Josie.
Josie who?
Josie who's at the door.

Knock–knock.

Who's there?
Juan.
Juan who?
Juan good turn
deserves another!

Knock–knock.

Who's there?
Juana.
Juana who?
Juana improve your
looks? Wear a mask.

Knock–knock.

Who's there?
Juarez.
Juarez who?
Juarez you hiding,
you rascal you?

Knock–knock.

Who's there?
Juan.
Juan who?
Juan two, buckle my shoe . . .

Knock–knock.

Who's there?
Grigor.
Grigor who?
Grigor (three, four),
shut the door . . .

Knock–knock.

Who's there?
Physics.
Physics who?
Physics (five, six), pick up sticks.

Knock–knock.

Who's there?
Stefan Haight.
Stefan Haight who?
Stefan Haight, lay them straight.

Knock–knock.

Who's there?
Jubilee.
Jubilee who?
Jubilee-ve in the tooth fairy?

Knock–knock.

Who's there?
Judah.
Judah who?
Judah known by now if you opened the door.

Knock–knock.

Who's there?
Juicy Watt.
Juicy Watt who?
Juicy Watt someone wrote on your door?

Knock–knock.

Who's there?
Jules.
Jules who?
Jules are in the safe.

Knock–knock.

Who's there?
Juliet.
Juliet who?
Juliet the cat out of the bag.

Knock–knock.

Who's there?
Junior.
Junior who?
Junior flowers will come up.

Knock–knock.

Who's there?
Juneau.
Juneau who?
Juneau what time it is?

Knock–knock.

Who's there?
Nome.
Nome who?
Nome, I don't.

Knock–knock.

Who's there?
Alaska.
Alaska who?
Alaska someone else.

Knock–knock.

Who's there?
Juno.
Juno who?
I don't know, Juno?

Knock–knock.

Who's there?
Jupiter.
Jupiter who?
Jupiter note on my door?

Knock–knock.

Who's there?
Jupiter.
Jupiter who?
Jupiter hurry or you'll miss
the garbage truck.

Knock–knock.

Who's there?
Justice.
Justice who?
Justice I got home the phone rang.

Knock–knock.

Who's there?
Justin.
Justin who?
Justin time for dinner.

Knock–knock.

Who's there?
Justine.
Justine who?
Justine old fashioned girl.

Knock–knock.

Who's there?
Justis.
Justis who?
Justis I thought.
Wrong door.

Knock–knock.

Who's there?
Karaoke.
Karaoke who?
Karaoke or not okay?

Knock–knock.

Who's there?
Kareem Cohen.
Kareem Cohen who?
Ice Kareem Cohen!

Knock–knock.

Who's there?
Karen.
Karen who?
Karen-teed to crack
you up!

Knock–knock.

Who's there?
Katmandu.
Katmandu who?
Katmandu what Catwoman
wants.

Knock–knock.

Who's there?
Keefe.
Keefe who?
Keefe me one more chance!

Knock–knock.

Who's there?
Keith.
Keith who?
Keith me, you fool!

Knock–knock.

Who's there?
Ken D.
Ken D. who?
Ken D. Gram.

Knock–knock.

Who's there?
Ken.
Ken who?
Ken I come in?
It's freezing out here.

Knock–knock.

Who's there?
Kenya.
Kenya who?
Kenya hear me knocking? I said
"knock-knock!"

Knock–knock.

Who's there?
Kenya.
Kenya who?
Kenya keep it down in there?

Knock–knock.

Who's there?
Kermit.
Kermit who?
Kermit me to introduce myself.

Knock–knock.

Who's there?
Ketchup.
Ketchup who?
Ketchup with me and I'll tell you.

Knock–knock.

Who's there?
Kevin.
Kevin who?
"Thank Kevin for little girls . . ."

Knock–knock.

Who's there?
Kiefer.
Kiefer who?
Kiefer stiff upper lip.

Knock–knock.

Who's there?
Kimono.
Kimono who?
Kimono my house.

Knock–knock.

Who's there?
King Kong.
King Kong who?
"King Kong, the witch
is dead . . ."

Knock–knock.

Who's there?
Kip.
Kip who?
Kip talking. Maybe
you'll find something
to say.

HEE
HEE

Knock–knock.

Who's there?
Kip.
   Kip who?
Kip your sunny side up.

Knock–knock.

Who's there?
Kipper.
   Kipper who?
Kipper hands to yourself.

Knock–knock.

Who's there?
Klaus.
   Klaus who?
Klaus your mouth
and open the door!

Knock–knock.

Who's there?
Knoxville.
   Knoxville who?
Knoxville get you an answer
if you wait long enough.

Knock–knock.

Who's there?
Koala.
   Koala who?
Koala-T jokes like these are
hard to find.

Knock–knock.

Who's there?
Kojak.
   Kojak who?
Kojak up the car.
We've got a flat.

Knock–knock.

Who's there?
Kokomo.
   Kokomo who?
Kokomo food—I'm hungry.

Knock–knock.

Who's there?
Krakatoa.
   Krakatoa who?
Just Krakatoa trying to kick
this door down!

Knock–knock.

Who's there?
Kris.
   Kris who?
Kris P. Critters!

Knock–knock.

Who's there?
Kumquat.
   Kumquat who?
Kumquat may, we'll always be buddies.

Knock–knock.

Who's there?
Kurt.
Kurt who?
Kurt that out!

Knock–knock.

Who's there?
Kurt and Conan.
Kurt and Conan who?
Kurt and Conan (curtain coming)
down on the last act.

Knock–knock.

Who's there?
Land.
    Land who?
It's "land-ho," not "land who."

Knock–knock.

Who's there?
Lava.
    Lava who?
"Lava, come back to me . . ."

Knock–knock.

Who's there?
L.B.
    L.B. who?
L.B. the judge of that!

Knock–knock.

Who's there?
Leah Penn.
    Leah Penn who?
Leah Penn Lizards!

Knock–knock.

Who's there?
Lee King.
Lee King who?
Lee King bucket.

Knock–knock.

Who's there?
Lemuel.
Lemuel who?
Lemuel kicked me.

Knock–knock.

Who's there?
Thor.
Thor who?
Thor all over.

Knock–knock.

Who's there?
Leonie.
Leonie who?
Leonie thing you do fast is get tired.

Knock–knock.

Who's there?
Leopold.
Leopold who?
Leopold the class and everyone
wants a new teacher.

Knock–knock.

Who's there?
Lester.
Lester who?
Lester the Red Hot Mamas.

Knock–knock.

Who's there?
Letter.
Letter who?
Letter smile be your umbrella.

Knock–knock.

Who's there?
Lettuce.
Lettuce who?
Lettuce discuss this like mature adults . . .

Knock–knock.

Who's there?
Lettuce.
Lettuce who?
Lettuce in and we'll tell you
another knock-knock joke.

Knock–knock.

Who's there?
Levin.
Levin who?
"Levin on a jet plane."

Knock–knock.

Who's there?
Lice.
Lice who?
Lice out by ten o'clock.

Knock–knock.

Who's there?
Lilac.
Lilac who?
Lilac that and you'll get punished.

Knock–knock.

Who's there?
Lima bean.
Lima bean who?
"Lima bean (I've been)
working on the railroad . . ."

Knock–knock.

Who's there?
Lion.
Lion who?
Lion here on your doorstep
till you open the door.

Knock–knock.

Who's there?
Linda.
Linda who?
Linda helping hand.

Knock–knock.

Who's there?
Yukon.
Yukon who?
Yukon count on me.

Knock–knock.

Who's there?
Lion.
Lion who?
Lion down on the job again?

Knock–knock.

Who's there?
Lionel.
Lionel who?
Lionel bite you if you
don't watch out.

Knock–knock.

Who's there?
Lionel.
Lionel who?
Lionel get you in trouble!

Knock–knock.

Who's there?
Lisa.
Lisa who?
Lisa you can do is let me in.

Knock–knock.

Who's there?
Little old lady.
Little old lady who?
I didn't know you could yodel.

Knock–knock.

Who's there?
Liv.
Liv who?
Liv no stone unturned.

Knock–knock.

Who's there?
Liver.
Liver who?
Liver round here?

Knock–knock.

Who's there?
Lotto.
Lotto who?
Lotto trouble coming your way if you don't open up.

Knock–knock.

Who's there?
Lucas Tell.
Lucas Tell who?
Lucas Tell-oh and Bud Abbott.

Knock–knock.

Who's there?
Lucinda.
Lucinda who?
Lucinda chain and let me inside.

Knock–knock.

Who's there?
Lucretia.
Lucretia who?
Lucretia (the creature) from the Black Lagoon.

HA!

Knock–knock.

Who's there?
Lucy.
Lucy who?
Lucy Nupp!

Knock–knock.

Who's there?
Lufthansa.
Lufthansa who?
Lufthansa! This is a stick-up!

Knock–knock.

Who's there?
Luigi.
Luigi who?
Luigi board.

Knock–knock.

Who's there?
Luke.
Luke who?
Luke before you leap.

Knock–knock.

Who's there?
Luke.
Luke who?
Luke through the keyhole and see.

Knock–knock.

Who's there?
Luke.
Luke who?
Luke out below!

Knock–knock.

Who's there?
Lyle.
Lyle who?
Lyle be a monkey's uncle!

Knock–knock.

Who's there?
Lyndon.
Lyndon who?
Lyndon ear and I'll tell you.

Scratch–scratch.

Who's there?
M-2.
M-2 who?
M-2 weak to knock.

Knock–knock.

Who's there?
Mabel.
Mabel who?
Mabel I'll tell you and Mabel I won't!

Knock–knock.

Who's there?
Mack.
Mack who?
Mack up your mind!

Knock–knock.

Who's there?
Macon.
Macon who?
"Macon a list, checking it twice."

Knock–knock.

Who's there?
Macon.
Macon who?
Macon whoopie.

Knock–knock.

Who's there?
Madge.
Madge who?
Madge N. that!

Knock–knock.

Who's there?
Madison.
Madison who?
You're Madison hatter!

Knock–knock.

Who's there?
Ma Harrison.
Ma Harrison who?
Ma Harrison (my hair is on) fire!

Knock–knock.

Who's there?
Major.
Major who?
Major bed, now lie in it.

Knock–knock.

Who's there?
Mamie.
Mamie who?
The Devil Mamie do it!

Knock–knock.

Who's there?
Mandalay.
Mandalay who?
Mandalay the kitchen tiles.

Knock–knock.

Who's there?
Mandy.
Mandy who?
Mandy lifeboats!
The ship is sinking!

Knock–knock.

Who's there?
Mannheim.
Mannheim who?
Mannheim tired!

Knock–knock.

Who's there?
Manny Dunn.
Manny Dunn who?
Manny Dunn grow on trees.

Knock–knock.

Who's there?
Mansion.
Mansion who?
Did I Mansion I have more
knock-knock jokes?

Knock–knock.

Who's there?
Marmoset.
Marmoset who?
Marmoset there'd be days like this.

Knock–knock.

Who's there?
Marsha.
Marsha who?
Marsha Mallow!

Knock–knock.

Who's there?
Mary and Abbey.
Mary and Abbey who?
Mary Christmas and Abbey New Year!

Knock–knock.

Who's there?
Massachusetts.

Massachusetts who?
Massachusetts is what you hear when a train blows its whistle.

Knock–knock.

Who's there?
Math.

Math who?
Math (mashed) potatoes!

Knock–knock.

Who's there?
Maude.

Maude who?
Maude as well go home.

Knock–knock.

Who's there?
Mavis.

Mavis who?
Mavis be the last time I knock at your door.

Knock–knock.

Who's there?
May Kay.
May Kay who?
May Kay while the sun shines!

Knock–knock.

Who's there?
Maynard.
Maynard who?
Maynard come around any-
more if you don't open up.

Knock–knock.

Who's there?
Mayonnaise.
Mayonnaise who?
"Mayonnaise be merry and bright . . ."

Knock–knock.

Who's there?
Mayonnaise.
Mayonnaise who?
"Mayonnaise have seen the glory
of the coming of the Lord . . ."

Knock–knock.

Who's there?
Mazda.
Mazda who?
Mazda of the Universe!

Knock–knock.

Who's there?
Megan.
Megan who?
Megan a phone call.

Knock–knock.

Who's there?
Jessamyn.
Jessamyn who?
Jessamyn-it please the
lion is busy.

Knock–knock.

Who's there?
Mustang.
Mustang who?
Mustang up now
I'm out of change.

Knock–knock.

Who's there?
Megan, Elise and Chicken.
Megan, Elise and Chicken who?
"He's Megan, Elise and Chicken it twice,
gonna find out who's naughty and nice . . ."

Knock–knock.

Who's there?
Me.
Me who?
Meow.

Knock–knock.

Who's there?
Melissa.
Melissa who?
Melissa to you and I get in trouble.

Knock–knock.

Who's there?
Melissa.
Melissa who?
Melissa longer than your list.

Knock–knock.

Who's there?
Menu.
Menu who?
Menu stay here, women over there.

Knock–knock.

Who's there?
Meteor.
Meteor who?
Prepare to Meteor (meet your) maker!

Knock–knock.

Who's there?
Meyer.
Meyer who?
Meyer in a nasty mood!

Knock–knock.

Who's there?
Michael Rhoda.
Michael Rhoda who?
"Michael Rhoda boat ashore, hallelujah . . ."

Knock–knock.

Who's there?
Michigan.
Michigan who?
"Michigan," said the batter
after the third strike.

Knock–knock.

Who's there?
Midas.
Midas who?
Midas well relax. I'm not going anyplace.

Knock–knock.

Who's there?
Midas.
Midas who?
Midas well try again—knock-knock!

...I'VE GOT THE **MIDAS** TOUCH!

Knock–knock.

Who's there?
Mike Rowe.
Mike Rowe who?
Mike Rowe wave oven.

Knock–knock.

Who's there?
Mike Howe.
Mike Howe who?
Mike Howe is sick.

Knock–knock.

Who's there?
Yvette.
Yvette who?
Yvette fixed her up.

Knock–knock.

Who's there?
Mimi.
Mimi who?
Mimi at the pool. I'd like to
give you drowning lessons.

Knock–knock.

Who's there?
Mindy.
Mindy who?
Mindy mood for pizza.

Knock–knock.

Who's there?
Nova.
Nova who?
Nova good place for pizza?

Knock–knock.

Who's there?
Noah.
Noah who?
Noah don't.

Knock–knock.

Who's there?
Newton.
Newton who?
Newton Monday, but I forgot.

Knock–knock.

Who's there?
Minerva.
Minerva who?
Minerva-s wreck from all these questions.

Knock–knock.

Who's there?
Miniature.
Miniature who?
Miniature open your mouth,
you put your foot in it.

Knock–knock.

Who's there?
Minna.
Minna who?
Minna wrong place at the
wrong time.

Knock–knock.

Who's there?
Minneapolis.
Minneapolis who?
Minneapolis each day keep
many doctors away.

Knock–knock.

Who's there?
Minnie.
Minnie who?
No, not Minnie-who–Minnehaha.

Knock–knock.

Who's there?
Mira.
Mira who?
Mira, Mira, on the wall.

Knock–knock.

Who's there?
Mischief.

Mischief who?
I guess I'd Mischief
(miss you if) you left . . .

Knock–knock.

Who's there?
Missouri.

Missouri who?
Missouri (misery)
loves company!

Knock–knock.

Who's there?
Mohair.

Mohair who?
Any Mohair on your
head and you could
pass for a mop.

Knock–knock.

Who's there?
Moose.

Moose who?
Moose beautiful girl in the world.

Knock–knock.

Who's there?
Monet.
Monet who?
Monet burns a hole in my pocket.

Knock–knock.

Who's there?
Morey and Les.
Morey and Les who?
The Morey I think of you,
the Les I think of you.

Knock–knock.

Who's there?
Morgan.
Morgan who?
Morgan just a pretty face!

Knock–knock.

Who's there?
Mrs. S. Goode.
Mrs. S. Goode who?
A Mrs. S. Goode as a mile.

Knock–knock.

Who's there?
Mr. T.
Mr. T. who?
"Ah, sweet Mr. T. of life . . ."

Knock–knock.

Who's there?
Murray Lee.
Murray Lee who?
"Murray Lee we roll along . . ."

Knock–knock.

Who's there?
Musket.
Musket who?
Musket in! The Martians are after me!

Knock–knock.

Who's there?
Mussolini.
Mussolini who?
Mussolini on your bell for ten minutes.

Knock–knock.

Who's there?
Mustard.
Mustard who?
Mustard been a beautiful baby.

Knock–knock.

Who's there?
Mustard Bean.
Mustard Bean who?
You Mustard Bean a big surprise
to your parents. They probably
expected a boy or girl.

Knock–knock.

Who's there?
Nanny.
Nanny who?
Nanny my friends like you either.

Knock–knock.

Who's there?
Nathan.
Nathan who?
Nathan to lose.

Knock–knock.

Who's there?
Nanya.
Nanya who?
Nanya Lip!

Knock–knock.

Who's there?
N.E.
N.E. who?
N.E. body you like, as long as you let me in!

Knock–knock.

Who's there?
Needle.
Needle who?
Needle little attention.

Knock–knock.

Who's there?
Needle.
Needle who?
Needle little help!

Knock–knock.

Who's there?
Nefertiti.
Nefertiti who?
Nefertiti (never teeter)
totter with a 500-pound gorilla!

Knock–knock.

Who's there?
Nemo.
Nemo who?
Nemo time to think of a joke!

Knock–knock.

Who's there?
Nestor.
Nestor who?
Nestor lives my neighbor.

Knock–knock.

Who's there?
Nevada.
Nevada who?
You Nevada had it so good!

Knock–knock.

Who's there?
Gouda.
Gouda who?
This is as Goudas it gets!

Knock–knock.

Who's there?
Osgood.
Osgood who?
Osgood S. Canby.

Knock–knock.

Who's there?
Nevil.
Nevil who?
Nevil mind!

Knock–knock.

Who's there?
Nevin.
Nevin who?
Nevin you mind—just open up.

Knock–knock.

Who's there?
Newark.
Newark who?
Newark for Noah.

Knock–knock.

Who's there?
Newark.
Newark who?
Newark keeps piling up.

Knock–knock.

Who's there?
New Year.
New Year who?
New Year (knew you were)
going to say that!

Knock–knock.

Who's there?
Noah.
Noah who?
There's Noah-scape!

Knock–knock.

Who's there?
Nobel.
Nobel who?
Nobel, so I knocked.

Knock–knock.

Who's there?
Noggin.
Noggin who?
Noggin at your door.

Knock–knock.

Who's there?
Noodle.
Noodle who?
Never Noodle now
where you lived.

Knock–knock.

Who's there?
Nora Marx.
Nora Marx who?
Nora Marx (no remarks) from
the peanut gallery!

Knock–knock.

Who's there?
Avery.
Avery who?
Avery body's gettin' into the act!

Knock–knock.

Who's there?
Norma Lee.
Norma Lee who?
Norma Lee I don't go around knocking on doors,
but I have this wonderful set of encyclopedias . . .

Knock–knock.

Who's there?
Notify.
Notify who?
Notify can help it.

Knock–knock.

Who's there?
Nova.
Nova who?
Nova look back.

Knock–knock.

Who's there?
Nuisance.
Nuisance who?
What's nuisance yesterday?

Knock–knock.

Who's there?
Nurse.
Nurse who?
Nurse sense in talking to you.

Knock–knock.

Who's there?
Nutmeg.
Nutmeg who?
Nutmeg any difference what you say.

Knock–knock.

Who's there?
O. A.
O. A. who?
"O. A. down South in Dixie."

Knock–knock.

Who's there?
Obi Wan.
Obi Wan who?
Obi Wan-derful and
take me to the movies!

Knock–knock.

Who's there?
O'Casey.
O'Casey who?
O'Casey if I care!

Knock–knock.

Who's there?
Occult.
Occult who?
Occult in my nose.

Knock–knock.

Who's there?
Ocelot.
  Ocelot who?
Ocelot of money for that.

Knock–knock.

Who's there?
Odaris.
  Odaris who?
Odaris a bee on your shoulder!

Knock–knock.

Who's there?
Odd Thing.
  Odd Thing who?
Odd Thing (I'd sing) all
day if I knew a thong!

Knock–knock.

Who's there?
Odysseus.
(Pronounced Oh-diss-us).
  Odysseus who?
Odysseus getting boring!

Knock–knock.

Who's there?
Odysseus.
  Odysseus who?
Odysseus the last straw!

Knock–knock.

Who's there?
Odyssey.
Odyssey who?
Odyssey (hard to see) how you
made it past the first grade!

Knock–knock.

Who's there?
Offer.
Offer who?
Offer got (I forgot)!

Knock–knock.

Who's there?
Office.
Office who?
He's Office rocker.

Knock–knock.

Who's there?
Ogre.
Ogre who?
Ogre take a flying leap!

Knock–knock.

Who's there?
Ohio.
Ohio who?
Ohio feeling?

Knock–knock.

Who's there?
Kentucky.
Kentucky who?
Kentucky (can't talk) too well,
have a sore throat.

Knock–knock.

Who's there?
Nevada.
Nevada who?
Nevada saw you look worse.
You should be in bed.

Knock–knock.

Who's there?
Ohio.
Ohio who?
Ohio Silver!

Knock–knock.

Who's there?
Ohio.
Ohio who?
Ohio than the highest mountain.

Knock–knock.

Who's there?
Oil well.
Oil well who?
Oil well that ends well.

Knock–knock.

Who's there?
Oink.
Oink who?
Oink L. Sam!

Knock–knock.

Who's there?
O'Keefe.
O'Keefe who?
"O'Keefe me a home
where the buffalo roam . . ."

Knock–knock.

Who's there?
Oklahoma.
Oklahoma who?
Oklahoma and wash your face.

Knock–knock.

Who's there?
Olaf.
Olaf who?
"Olaf My Heart in San Francisco."

Knock–knock.

Who's there?
Olga.
Olga who?
Olga home if you
don't treat me better.

Knock–knock.

Who's there?
Olivia.
Olivia who?
Olivia (I live here) but I forgot my key.

Knock–knock.

Who's there?
One door.
One door who?
One door where you are tonight.

Knock–knock.

Who's there?
Olivia.
Olivia who?
Olivia lone if that's what you want!

Knock–knock.

Who's there?
Olivia.
Olivia who?
Olivia me alone!

Knock–knock.

Who's there?
Ollie-Lou.
Ollie-Lou who?
Ollie-Lou ya! You finally
opened the door!

Knock–knock.

Who's there?
Ollie.
Ollie who?
Ollie time you say that,
I wish you'd cut it out.

Knock–knock.

Who's there?
Ollie or Rex.
Ollie or Rex who?
Don't put Ollie or Rex
in one basket.

Knock–knock.

Who's there?
Omaha.
Omaha who?
Omaha goodness! My hand
is caught in the door!

Knock–knock.

Who's there?
Omar.
Omar who?
Omar goodness gracious!
Wrong door!

Knock–knock.

Who's there?
Omega.
Omega who?
Omega best man win!

Knock–knock.

Who's there?
Omega.
Omega who?
Omega up your mind.

Knock–knock.

Who's there?
Ooze.
Ooze who?
Ooze in charge around here?

Knock–knock.

Who's there?
Opel.
Opel who?
Opel of mine.

Knock–knock.

Who's there?
Opossum.
Opossum who?
Opossum by and
thought I'd say hello.

Knock–knock.

Who's there?
Orange shoe.
Orange shoe who?
Orange shoe going to let me in?

Knock–knock.

Who's there?
Orangutan.
Orangutan who?
Orangutan times but
you didn't answer.

Knock–knock.

Who's there?
Orbach.
Orbach who?
Front Orbach—you look awful.

Knock–knock.

Who's there?
Oregon.
Oregon who?
Oregon and I'm not coming back.

Knock–knock.

Who's there?
Orson.
Orson who?
Orson buggy—want a ride?

Knock–knock.

Who's there?
Osborne.
Osborne who?
Osborne in the hospital.

Knock–knock.

Who's there?
Osgood.
Osgood who?
Osgood as it gets.

Knock–knock.

Who's there?
Oscar and Greta.
Oscar and Greta who?
Oscar foolish question and
Greta a foolish answer.

Knock–knock.

Who's there?
Osaka.
Osaka who?
Osaka to me!

Knock–knock.

Who's there?
Oxford.
Oxford who?
You Oxford it! (*Pow!*)

Knock–knock.

Who's there?
O'Shea.
O'Shea who?
O'Shea it isn't so.

Knock–knock.

Who's there?
Oslo.
Oslo who?
Oslo on cash.
How about a little loan?

Knock–knock.

Who's there?
Oslo.
Oslo who?
Oslo down, you're going too fast.

Knock–knock.

Who's there?
Oswego.
Oswego who?
"Oswego into the wild blue yonder."

Knock–knock.

Who's there?
Otter.
Otter who?
Otter apologize for these bad jokes.

Knock–knock.

Who's there?
Otto B.
Otto B. who?
Otto B. a law against people like you.

Knock–knock.

Who's there?
Otto.
Otto who?
Your bell is Otto order.

Knock–knock.

Who's there?
O. Verdi.
O. Verdi who?
"O. Verdi Rainbow."

Knock–knock.

Who's there?
Owen Williams.
Owen Williams who?
Owen Williams
(oh, when will you) open this door?

Knock–knock.

Who's there?
Owls.
Owls who?
You got it right this time.

Knock–knock.

Who's there?
Oz.
Oz who?
Oz out here freezing.

Knock–knock.

Who's there?
Paddy.
Paddy who?
Paddy your own canoe.

Knock–knock.

Who's there?
Pakistan.
Pakistan who?
Pakistan lunch. He's working late.

Knock–knock.

Who's there?
Pasadena.
Pasadena who?
Stop when you Pasadena—I'm hungry.

Knock–knock.

Who's there?
Passion.
Passion who?
Passion by and thought I'd say hello.

Knock–knock.

Who's there?
Panda.
Panda who?
Panda monium!

Knock–knock.

Who's there?
Pasta.
Pasta who?
Pasta pizza under the door—I'm starved!

Knock–knock.

Who's there?
Azenauer.
Azenauer who?
Azenauer (has an hour) gone by since you put the pizza in the oven?

Knock–knock.

Who's there?
Pasteur.
Pasteur who?
It's Pasteur (past your) bedtime!

Knock–knock.

Who's there?
Pasteurize.

Pasteurize who?
Pasteurize and over the gums,
look out stomach, here it comes.

Knock–knock.

Who's there?
Patella.

Patella who?
Patella story before bedtime.

Knock–knock.

Who's there?
Patton.

Patton who?
Patton leather shoes!

Knock–knock.

Who's there?
Paul.

Paul who?
Paul-tergeist!

Knock–knock.

Who's there?
Paula.

Paula who?
Paula few strings for me.

Knock–knock.

Who's there?
Pawtucket.

Pawtucket who?
I had a dollar, but Pawtucket.

Knock–knock.

Who's there?
Pay cents.

Pay cents who?
Pay cents is a virtue.

Knock–knock.

Who's there?
Peapod.

Peapod who?
I don't want to hear a Peapod
(peep out of) you!

Knock–knock.

Who's there?
Peekaboo.

Peekaboo who?
Peekaboo live in glass houses
shouldn't throw stones.

Knock–knock.

Who's there?
Pekingese.

Pekingese who?
Pekingese through the
peephole and see.

Knock–knock.

Who's there?
Peking.
Peking who?
Peking is not allowed.

Knock–knock.

Who's there?
Pembroke.
Pembroke who?
Pembroke, can I use yours?

Knock–knock.

Who's there?
Percy.
Percy who?
Percy-veere (persevere)!

Knock–knock.

Who's there?
Phineas.
Phineas who?
Phineas thing happened on
the way over here . . .

Knock–knock.

Who's there?
Phyllis.
Phyllis who?
Phyllis in on the details!

Knock–knock.

Who's there?
Picture.
Picture who?
Picture favorite flowers.

Knock–knock.

Who's there?
Pinafore.
Pinafore who?
Pinafore for your thoughts . . .

Knock–knock.

Who's there?
Pitcher.
Pitcher who?
Pitcher money where your mouth is!

Knock–knock.

Who's there?
Pizza.
Pizza who?
Pizza nice guy when you get
to know him.

Knock–knock.

Who's there?
Plate.

Plate who?
"Plate again, Sam."

Knock–knock.

Who's there?
Plato.

Plato who?
Plato spaghetti and meatballs, please.

Knock–knock.

Who's there?
Poker.

Poker who?
Poker Hontas.

Knock–knock.

Who's there?
Poland.

Poland who?
Poland or rich country?

Knock–knock.

Who's there?
Police.
Police who?
Police open the door!

Knock–knock.

Who's there?
Police.
Police who?
Police B. Careful!

Knock–knock.

Who's there?
Polly N.
Polly N. who?
Polly N. saturated.

Knock–knock.

Who's there?
Porsche.
Porsche who?
Porsche me in the
right direction!

Knock–knock.

Who's there?
Possum.
Possum who?
Possum peace pipe.

Knock–knock.

Who's there?
Preston.
Preston who?
Preston the doorbell,
but it won't ring.

Knock–knock.

Who's there?
Pumpkin.
Pumpkin who?
A thing that goes
pumpkin (bump in) the night.

Knock–knock.

Who's there?
Pudding.
Pudding who?
Pudding my best foot forward!

Knock–knock.

Who's there?
Punch.
Punch who?
Not me—I just got here!

Knock–knock.

Who's there?
Pyrite.
Pyrite who?
Pyrite in your face—Pow!

Knock–knock.

Who's there?
Quaint.
Quaint who?
"Quaint nothing but a hound dog."

Knock–knock.

Who's there?
Quake.
Quake who?
Quake up, you sleepyhead.

Knock–knock.

Who's there?
Que Sarah.
Que Sarah who?
"Que Sarah, Sarah; whatever
will be, will be."

Knock–knock.

Who's there?
Quibble.
Quibble who?
Quibble and Bits.

Knock–knock.

Who's there?
Quiet Tina.
Quiet Tina who?
Quiet Tina courtroom—monkey wants to speak.

Knock–knock.

Who's there?
Quigley.
Quigley who?
Open the door Quigley, I must get in!

Knock–knock.

Who's there?
Radio.
Radio who?
Radio not, here I come!

Knock–knock.

Who's there?
Raisin.
Raisin who?
Raisin Cane!

Knock–knock.

Who's there?
Rajah.
Rajah who?
Rajah Rabbit!

Knock–knock.

Who's there?
Ralph.
Ralph who?
Ralph! Ralph! I'm a puppy dog!

Knock–knock.

Who's there?
Rambo.
Rambo who?
"Somewhere, over the Rambo . . ."

Knock–knock.

Who's there?
Ramona.
Ramona who?
Ramona going to ask you once more . . .

Knock–knock.

Who's there?
Randall.
Randall who?
Randall the way from the bus.

Knock–knock.

Who's there?
Randy and Vanna.
Randy and Vanna who?
Randy race and Vanna medal.

Knock–knock.

Who's there?
Raoul (pronounced Rah-*ool*).
Raoul who?
"Raoul out the barrel . . ."

Knock–knock.

Who's there?
Raptor.
Raptor who?
Raptor presents before Christmas.

Knock–knock.

Who's there?
A Raven.
A Raven who?
A Raven Maniac.

Knock–knock.

Who's there?
Ray and Greta.
Ray and Greta who?
You'll Ray Greta asking me that!

Knock–knock.

Who's there?
Rector.
Rector who?
Rector car. Can I use your phone?

Knock–knock.

Who's there?
Renata.
Renata who?
Renata (run out of) steam?

Knock–knock.

Who's there?
Reverend.
Reverend who?
For Reverend ever I've
been standing out here . . .

Knock–knock.

Who's there?
Rhett.
Rhett who?
Rhett-urn of the Jedi.

Knock–knock.

Who's there?
Rhonda.
Rhonda who?
Rhonda arrest!

Knock–knock.

Who's there?
Rhoda.
Rhoda who?
Rhoda dendron.

Knock–knock.

Who's there?
Rich.
Rich who?
Rich way did he go?

Knock–knock.

Who's there?
Rick.
Rick who?
Rick Shaw, hop in for a ride!

Knock–knock.

Who's there?
Ringo.
Ringo who?
Ringo round the collar.

Knock–knock.

Who's there?
Ripon.
Ripon who?
Ripon up your welcome mat.

Knock–knock.

Who's there?
Rise and Follow.
Rise and Follow who?
Rise and Follow (rise and fall of) the Roman Empire.

Knock–knock.

Who's there?
Rita.
Rita who?
Rita my lips!

Knock–knock.

Who's there?
Robert de Niro.
Robert de Niro who?
Robert de Niro, but he's not here yet.

Knock–knock.

Who's there?
Robert Redford.
Robert Redford who?
Robert Redford the part in the play.

Knock–knock.

Who's there?
Robin.
Robin who?
Robin you! Hand over your money!

Knock–knock.

Who's there?
Roger.
Roger who?
Roger. Over and out.

Knock–knock.

Who's there?
Rollin.
Rollin who?
"As we come rollin' rollin' home . . ."

Knock–knock.

Who's there?
Roman.
Roman who?
Roman around with nothing to do.

Knock–knock.

Who's there?
Romanoff.
Romanoff who?
There ain't Romanoff for the
both of us in this town!

Knock–knock.

Who's there?
Ronan.
Ronan who?
Ronan amuck!

Knock–knock.

Who's there?
Ron.
Ron who?
Ron for your life!

Knock–knock.

Who's there?
Rover.
Rover who?
It's all Rover between us.

Knock–knock.

Who's there?
Roxanne.
Roxanne who?
Roxanne your head or something?

Knock–knock.

Who's there?
Rona.
Rona who?
Rona the mill.

HEE
HEE

Knock–knock.

Who's there?
Roy.
Roy who?
Roy L. Flush!

Knock–knock.

Who's there?
Rubber.
Rubber who?
Rubber the wrong way and
she'll smack you.

Knock–knock.

Who's there?
Rubber Duck.
Rubber Duck who?
"Rubber Duck dub–three men in a tub . . ."

Knock–knock.

Who's there?
Rufus.
Rufus who?
Rufus leaking and I'm getting wet.

Knock–knock.

Who's there?
Rumania.
Rumania who?
Can't Rumania out here much longer.

Knock–knock.

Who's there?
Russ.
Russ who?
Russ Crispies!

Knock–knock.

Who's there?
Sadie.

Sadie who?
Sadie Pledge of Allegiance.

Knock–knock.

Who's there?
Safari.

Safari who?
Safari so good.

Knock–knock.

Who's there?
Safaris.

Safaris who?
Safaris I can see, it's me!

Knock–knock.

Who's there?
Salada.

Salada who?
Salada bad knock-knock
jokes around.

Knock–knock.

Who's there?
Salem.
Salem who?
Salem away for good—never
have to see you again.

Knock–knock.

Who's there?
Salome.
Salome who?
Salome on rye with mustard.

Knock–knock.

Who's there?
Sam and Janet.
Sam and Janet who?
"Sam and Janet evening,
you will meet a stranger . . ."

Knock–knock.

Who's there?
Sam.
Sam who?
Sam old story. Ho-hum.

Knock–knock.

Who's there?
Samovar.
Samovar who?
Samovar time you can be a real pest.

2001 Knock–Knocks & Tongue Twisters

Knock–knock.

Who's there?
Sancho.
Sancho who?
Sancho a letter, but
you never answered.

Knock–knock.

Who's there?
Sanctuary.
Sanctuary who?
Sanctuary much.

Knock–knock.

Who's there?
Santa Ana.
Santa Ana who?
Santa Ana coming
to your house because
you've been bad.

Knock–knock.

Who's there?
Santa.
Santa who?
Santa Mental Fool!

Knock–knock.

Who's there?
Santucci.
Santucci who?
Santucci my sunburn!

Knock–knock.

Who's there?
Sarah.
Sarah who?
Sarah doorbell around here?
I'm tired of knocking.

Knock–knock.

Who's there?
Sarah.
Sarah who?
Sarah doctor in the house?

Knock–knock.

Who's there?
Sarong and Sari.
Sarong and Sari who?
Sarong house. Sari.

Knock–knock.

Who's there?
Sarasota.
Sarasota who?
Sarasota in the fridge? I'm thirsty.

Knock–knock.

Who's there?
Sari.
Sari who?
Sari, wrong number.

Knock–knock.

Who's there?
Sasha.
Sasha who?
Sasha dummy!

Knock–knock.

Who's there?
Satin.
Satin who?
Who Satin my chair?

Knock–knock.

Who's there?
Satellite.
Satellite who?
Satellite in the window—one
if by land, two if by sea.

Knock–knock.

Who's there?
Saul and Terry.
Saul and Terry who?
Saul and Terry confinement!

Knock–knock.

Who's there?
Schick.
Schick who?
I'm Schick as a dog.

Knock–knock.

Who's there?
Esau.
Esau who?
Esau throat is killing me.

Knock–knock.

Who's there?
Consuelo.
Consuelo who?
Consuelo a thing.

Knock–knock.

Who's there?
Gargoyle.
Gargoyle who?
Gargoyle with salt water
and you'll feel better.

Knock–knock.

Who's there?
Hatch.
Hatch who?
I didn't know you were
sick, too.

Knock–knock.

Who's there?
Saul Upp.
Saul Upp who?
Saul Upp to you!

Knock–knock.

Who's there?
Sauna.
Sauna who?
"Sauna clear day you can see forever."

Knock–knock.

Who's there?
Schatzi.
Schatzi who?
Schatzi way the ball bounces.

Knock–knock.

Who's there?
Schenectady.
Schenectady who?
Schenectady plug to the socket.

Knock–knock.

Who's there?
Schenectady.
Schenectady who?
Schenectady (the neck
of the) shirt is too tight.

Knock–knock.

Who's there?
Scissor.
Scissor who?
Scissor and Cleopatra.

Knock–knock.

Who's there?
Scissors.
Scissors who?
Scissors lovely way to spend the evening.

Knock–knock.

Who's there?
Scoot.
Scoot who?
Scoot to be here!

Knock–knock.

Who's there?
Scold.
Scold who?
Scold outside.

Knock–knock.

Who's there?
Scott.
  Scott who?
Scott to be me!

Knock–knock.

Who's there?
Sea Bass.
  Sea Bass who?
Sea Bass-tian the crab.

Knock–knock.

Who's there?
Seashell.
  Seashell who?
"Seashell have music wherever she goes . . ."

Knock–knock.

Who's there?
Sedimentary.
  Sedimentary who?
Sedimentary, my dear Watson.

Knock–knock.

Who's there?
Seiko.
  Seiko who?
"Seiko and ye shall find . . ."

Knock–knock.

Who's there?
Seminole.
Seminole who?
"Seminole cowhand—
from the Rio Grande . . ."

Knock–knock.

Who's there?
Senior.
Senior who?
Senior through the peephole,
so I know you're in there.

Knock–knock.

Who's there?
Serbia.
Serbia who?
Serbia yourself.

Knock–knock.

Who's there?
Seth.
Seth who?
Seth me, that's who.

Knock–knock.

Who's there?
Sew.
Sew who?
Sew what else is new?

Knock–knock.

Who's there?
Seymour.
Seymour who?
Seymour if you'd get the door open.

Knock–knock.

Who's there?
Sharon.
Sharon who?
Sharon share alike.

Knock–knock.

Who's there?
Shafter.
Shafter who?
Shafter make a phone call!

Knock–knock.

Who's there?
Sheila.
Sheila who?
"Sheila be coming
round the mountain
when she comes . . ."

Knock–knock.

Who's there?
Shirley M.
Shirley M. who?
Shirley M. glad to say
goodbye to you.

Knock–knock.

Who's there?
Shirley.
Shirley who?
Shirley you know my name.

Knock–knock.

Who's there?
Shelley.
Shelley who?
Shelley try again?

Knock–knock.

Who's there?
Dozen.
Dozen who?
Dozen matter to me!

Knock–knock.

Who's there?
Shoe buckle.
Shoe buckle who?
Shoe buckle up your seat belt?

Knock–knock.

Who's there?
Shoes.
Shoes who?
Shoes me, I must have
knocked on the wrong door.

Knock–knock.

Who's there?
Shopper Dan.
Shopper Dan who?
You're Shopper Dan
(sharper than) I thought!

Knock–knock.

Who's there?
Siam.
Siam who?
Siam your old pal.

Knock–knock.

Who's there?
Siamese.
Siamese who?
Siamese-y to please.

Knock–knock.

Who's there?
Sid.
Sid who?
"Sid-down, you're
rocking the boat . . ."

Knock–knock.

Who's there?
Sigrid.
Sigrid who?
Sigrid Service—open up!

Knock–knock.

Who's there?
Simmer.
Simmer who?
"Simmer time and the living is easy."

Knock–knock.

Who's there?
Simms.
Simms who?
Simms like I'm always knocking on doors.

Knock–knock.

Who's there?
Simon.
Simon who?
"Simon the mood for love . . ."

Knock–knock.

Who's there?
Sinatra.

Sinatra who?
Sinatra the cough that carries you off, it's the coffin they carry you off in.

Knock–knock.

Who's there?
Sincerely.

Sincerely who?
Sincerely this morning I've been listening to knock-knock jokes.

Knock–knock.

Who's there?
Singapore.

Singapore who?
Singapore song or a rich song.

Knock–knock.

Who's there?
Sis.

Sis who?
Sis any way to treat a friend?

HEE
HEE

Knock–knock.

Who's there?
Sizzle.
Sizzle who?
Sizzle be my shining hour.

Knock–knock.

Who's there?
Slater.
Slater who?
Slater than you think.

Knock–knock.

Who's there?
Sloan.
Sloan who?
Sloan (slow and) steady wins the race!

Knock–knock.

Who's there?
Sly Dover.
Sly Dover who?
Sly Dover, I'm breaking down the door!

Knock–knock.

Who's there?
Snow.
Snow who?
Snow use talking to you.

Knock–knock.

Who's there?
Snow.

Snow who?
Snow use using the doorbell,
it's broken.

Knock–knock.

Who's there?
Sodium.

Sodium who?
Sodium (so do you) mind if
I come in?

Knock–knock.

Who's there?
Sony.

Sony who?
Sony your old pal . . .

Knock–knock.

Who's there?
Trotter.

Trotter who?
Trotter remember me.

Knock–knock.

Who's there?
Sonny N.

Sonny N. who?
Sonny N. clear today—rain tomorrow!

Knock–knock.

Who's there?
Sony and Toshiba.
Sony and Toshiba who?
Sony me, waiting Toshiba.

Knock–knock.

Who's there?
Spetzel.
Spetzel who?
Spetzel delivery!

Knock–knock.

Who's there?
Spook.
Spook who?
I spook too soon!

Knock–knock.

Who's there?
Stan.
Stan who?
Stan back—I'm knocking the
door down.

Knock–knock.

Who's there?
Stark.
Stark who?
Stark in here, turn on the light.

S

Knock–knock.

Who's there?
Statue.
Statue who?
Statue in there?

Knock–knock.

Who's there?
Stan and Bea.
Stan and Bea who?
Stan Dupp and Bea Counted!

Knock–knock.

Who's there?
Stella.
Stella who?
Stella no answer at the door.

Knock–knock.

Who's there?
Stencil.
Stencil who?
Stencil—there's a bee on
your nose.

Knock–knock.

Who's there?
Stephen.
Stephen who?
Stephen out with my baby.

Knock–knock.

Who's there?
Stephen.
Stephen who?
Stephen the gas.

Knock–knock.

Who's there?
Stu.
Stu who?
Stu darn hot.

Knock–knock.

Who's there?
Stu.
Stu who?
Stu late now.

Knock–knock.

Who's there?
Sue.
Sue who?
Sue-prise–it's me!

Knock–knock.

Who's there?
Sumatra.
Sumatra who?
What's Sumatra with you?

Knock–knock.

Who's there?
Surreal.

Surreal who?
Surreal pleasure to be here!

Knock–knock.

Who's there?
Sven.

Sven who?
Sven are you going
to open the door?

Knock–knock.

Who's there?
Swann.

Swann who?
"Just Swann of those things . . ."

Knock–knock.

Who's there?
Swatter.

Swatter who?
Swatter you complaining
about now?

Knock–knock.

Who's there?
Sybil.

Sybil who?
Sybil War!

Knock–knock.

Who's there?
Sycamore.

Sycamore who?
Sycamore knock-knock jokes.

Knock–knock.

Who's there?
Tamara.
Tamara who?
Tamara Boom-dee-ay!

Knock–knock.

Who's there?
Tara.
Tara who?
"Tara-ra-boom-ti-ay."

Knock–knock.

Who's there?
Tanya.
Tanya who?
Tanya come out and play?

Knock–knock.

Who's there?
Tarragon.
Tarragon who?
Tarragon with the wind.

Knock–knock.

Who's there?
Tarzan.
Tarzan who?
Tarzan feather 'em.

Knock–knock.

Who's there?
Tasmania.
Tasmania who?
Tasmania slip between the cup and the lip.

Knock–knock.

Who's there?
Taurus.
Taurus who?
Taurus closed on my foot. Ouch!

Knock–knock.

Who's there?
Taylor.
Taylor who?
Taylor I can't make it.

Knock–knock.

Who's there?
Tennessee.
Tennessee who?
Is that a Tennessee (tan I see),
or haven't you bathed lately?

Knock–knock.

Who's there?
Tennessee.
Tennessee who?
Tennessee you tonight?

Knock–knock.

Who's there?
Tamara.
Tamara who?
Tamara would be better.

Knock–knock.

Who's there?
Terrify.
Terrify who?
Terrify tissue?

Knock–knock.

Who's there?
Tess Slater.
Tess Slater who?
Tess Slater than you think!

Knock–knock.

Who's there?
Thaddeus.
Thaddeus who?
Thaddeus the silliest
thing I ever heard.

Knock–knock.

Who's there?
Thayer.
Thayer who?
Thayer thorry and I won't
throw this pie in your face.

Knock–knock.

Who's there?
Thea.
Thea who?
Thea later, alligator.

Knock–knock.

Who's there?
Thee.
Thee who?
Thee old gray mare.

Knock–knock.

Who's there?
Thelonius.
Thelonius who?
Thelonius kid in town.

Knock–knock.

Who's there?
The Genius.
    The Genius who?
The Genius (the genie is)
out of the bottle.

Knock–knock.

Who's there?
The Ghost.
    The Ghost who?
The Ghost is clear—let's go!

Knock–knock.

Who's there?
Theodore.
    Theodore who?
Theodore is closed, open up!

Knock–knock.

Who's there?
Theonie.
    Theonie who?
Theonie trouble with
your face is that it shows.

Knock–knock.

Who's there?
Theophilus.
    Theophilus who?
Theophilus person I ever met is you.

Knock–knock.

Who's there?
Theresa.
Theresa who?
Theresa crowd.

Knock–knock.

Who's there?
Theresa.
Theresa who?
Theresa fly in my soup.

Knock–knock.

Who's there?
Thistle.
Thistle who?
Thistle be the last time I knock on your door.

Knock–knock.

Who's there?
Thistle.
Thistle who?
Thistle teach you not to ask
silly questions.

Knock–knock.

Who's there?
Threadbare.
   Threadbare who?
Threadbare-n (the Red Baron)
and Snoopy the Flying Ace.

Knock–knock.

Who's there?
Thud.
   Thud who?
Thud you'd never ask!

Knock–knock.

Who's there?
Thurston.
   Thurston who?
Thurston for some water.

Knock–knock.

Who's there?
Tibet.
   Tibet who?
Early Tibet and early to rise . . .

Knock–knock.

Who's there?
Tick.
   Tick who?
Tick 'em up!

Knock–knock.

Who's there?
Tijuana.
Tijuana who?
Tijuana try for two out of three?

Knock–knock.

Who's there?
Tinker Bell.
Tinker Bell who?
Tinker Bell is out of order.

Knock–knock.

Who's there?
Tissue.
Tissue who?
Tissue were here.

Knock–knock.

Who's there?
Titus.
Titus who?
Titus a drum.

Knock–knock.

Who's there?
Titus.
Titus who?
Titus string around your finger so you
won't forget to open the door.

Knock–knock.

Who's there?
Toad.
Toad who?
Toad you before, but you forgot.

Knock–knock.

Who's there?
Tobacco.
Tobacco who?
Tobacco your car you have
to put it in reverse.

Knock–knock.

Who's there?
Toboggan.
Toboggan who?
Yes, but I don't like Toboggan.

Knock–knock.

Who's there?
Tobias.
Tobias who?
Are you going Tobias more
knock-knock books?

Knock–knock.

Who's there?
Toby.
Toby who?
Toby or not Toby.

Knock–knock.

Who's there?
Thaddeus.
Thaddeus who?
Thaddeus question.

Knock–knock.

Who's there?
Tobias.
Tobias who?
Tobias you need a lot of money.

Knock–knock.

Who's there?
Toby.
Toby who?
Toby continued.

Knock–knock.

Who's there?
Toledo.
Toledo who?
It's easy Toledo horse to water,
but you can't make him drink.

Knock–knock.

Who's there?
Tom Hills.
Tom Hills who?
Tom Hills (time heals) all wounds!

Knock–knock.

Who's there?
Tommy.
Tommy who?
I have a Tommy Ache!

Knock–knock.

Who's there?
Toodle-oo.
Toodle-oo who?
"Skip Toodle-oo, my darling . . ."

Knock–knock.

Who's there?
Toodle.
Toodle who?
Bye-bye.

Knock–knock.

Who's there?
Toothache.
Toothache who?
Toothache the high road
and I'll take the low road.

Knock–knock.

Who's there?
Top Hat.
  Top Hat who?
Top Hat (stop that—
you're bothering me!)

Knock–knock.

Who's there?
Topeka.
  Topeka who?
Don't open the door. I like
Topeka through keyholes.

Knock–knock.

Who's there?
Topol.
  Topol who?
"On Topol Old Smokey . . ."

Knock–knock.

Who's there?
Toreador.
  Toreador who?
Toreador down—now can
I come in?

Knock–knock.

Who's there?
Toulouse.
  Toulouse who?
Want Toulouse ten ugly
pounds? Cut off your head.

Knock–knock.

Who's there?
Toronto.
Toronto who?
Have Toronto the store.
Can I get you anything?

Knock–knock.

Who's there?
Canada.
Canada who?
Canada best dog food.

Knock–knock.

Who's there?
T. Rex.
T. Rex who?
T. Rex your appetite more than coffee.

Knock–knock.

Who's there?
Trigger.
Trigger who?
Trigger treat!

Knock–knock.

Who's there?
Troy.
Troy who?
Troy as I may, I can't reach the bell.

Knock–knock.

Who's there?
Troy.
Troy who?
Troy again!

Knock–knock.

Who's there?
Wes D.
Wes D. who?
Wes D. point?

Knock–knock.

Who's there?
Trudy.
Trudy who?
Can I come Trudy window?
The door is stuck.

Knock–knock.

Who's there?
Truman E.
Truman E. who?
Truman E. cooks spoil the broth!

Knock–knock.

Who's there?
Turner.
Turner who?
Turner round. You look
better from the back.

Knock–knock.

Who's there?
Turnip.
Turnip who?
Turnip the volume. I can't hear.

Knock–knock.

Who's there?
Twain.
Twain who?
Twain on track nine.

Knock–knock.

Who's there?
Two badgers.
Two badgers who?
Two badgers got a chip on your shoulder.

Knock–knock.

Who's there?
Typhoid.
Typhoid who?
Typhoid you were looking for me.

Knock–knock.

Who's there?
U-Boat.
U-Boat who?
U-Boat me a present?

Knock–knock.

Who's there?
Udall.
Udall who?
Udall know if you
opened the door.

Knock–knock.

Who's there?
Udder.
Udder who?
Udder Lee ridiculous!

Knock–knock.

Who's there?
Uganda.
Uganda who?
Uganda be kidding me!

Knock–knock.

Who's there?
Uganda.
Uganda who?
Uganda get away with this.

Knock–knock.

Who's there?
Uganda.
Uganda who?
Uganda never guess.

Knock–knock.

Who's there?
Uma.
Uma who?
"Uma Darling Clementine."

Knock–knock.

Who's there?
Unique.
Unique who?
Why do Unique (you sneak)
around on tiptoe?

Knock–knock.

Who's there?
Unaware.
Unaware who?
Your unaware has a hole in it!

Knock–knock.

Who's there?
Tom Sawyer.
Tom Sawyer who?
Tom Sawyer underwear.

Knock–knock.

Who's there?
Arkansas.
Arkansas who?
Arkansas it, too!

Knock–knock.

Who's there?
Esau.
Esau who?
Esau it too.

Knock–knock.

Who's there?
Unicorn.
Unicorn who?
Unicorn-iest guy I ever met.

Knock–knock.

Who's there?
Upton.
Upton who?
Upton Sesame.

Knock–knock.

Who's there?
Unity.
Unity who?
Unity sweater for me?

Knock–knock.

Who's there?
Upton.
Upton who?
Upton no good, as usual.

Knock–knock.

Who's there?
Uriah.
Uriah who?
Keep Uriah on the ball.

Knock–knock.

Who's there?
Ural.
Ural who?
Ural washed up, kid!

Knock–knock.

Who's there?
Uruguay.
Uruguay who?
You go Uruguay and I'll go mine.

Knock–knock.

Who's there?
Usher.
Usher who?
Usher wish you would let me in.

Knock–knock.

Who's there?
U-turn.
U-turn who?
U-turn my legs to jelly.

Knock–knock.

Who's there?
Uta.
Uta who?
Uta sight, uta mind.

Knock–knock.

Who's there?
Uta May.
Uta May who?
Going Uta May mind!

Knock–knock.

Who's there?
Utah-Nevada.
Utah-Nevada who?
Utah-Nevada guessed if
I didn't tell you.

Knock–knock.

Who's there?
Utica.
Utica who?
Utica high road and I'll
take the low road.

Knock–knock.

Who's there?
Vacancy.
Vacancy who?
Vacancy (we can see)
right in your window!

Knock–knock.

Who's there?
Valley.
Valley who?
Valley intellesting!

Knock–knock.

Who's there?
Vanna.
Vanna who?
Vanna go to the movies?

Knock–knock.

Who's there?
Vanna White.
Vanna White who?
Vanna White (want to write)
your name on this dotted line?

Knock–knock.

Who's there?
Vasilli.
Vasilli who?
Vasilli (what a silly) person you are!

Knock–knock.

Who's there?
Van Gogh.
Van Gogh who?
Ready–set–Van Gogh!

Knock–knock.

Who's there?
Vassar girl.
Vassar girl who?
Vassar girl like you doing in a place like this?

Knock–knock.

Who's there?
Vaudeville.
Vaudeville who?
Vaudeville (what will) you be doing tonight?

Knock–knock.

Who's there?
Vaughan.
Vaughan who?
"Vaughan day my prince will come . . ."

Knock–knock.

Who's there?
Vaughan.
Vaughan who?
Vaughan to come over tomorrow?

Knock–knock.

Who's there?
Veal chop.
Veal chop who?
Veal chop for a used car.

Knock–knock.

Who's there?
Vehicle.
Vehicle who?
Don't call us—Vehicle (we will call) you!

Knock–knock

Who's there?
Venice.
Venice who?
Venice these knock-knock
jokes going to stop?

Knock–knock.

Who's there?
Ventriloquist.
Ventriloquist who?
Ventriloquist-mas tree get decorated?

Knock–knock.

Who's there?
Venus.
Venus who?
Venus see you, I feel sick.

Knock–knock.

Who's there?
Verdi.
Verdi who?
Verdi wave goes, so goes the surfer.

Knock–knock.

Who's there?
Veronica.
Veronica who?
Veronica (we're on a c-)razy diet.

Knock–knock.

Who's there?
Vera.
Vera who?
"Vera all the flowers gone . . ."

Knock–knock.

Who's there?
Vespucci.
Vespucci who?
How much is Vespucci (that poochie) in the window?

Knock–knock.

Who's there?
Vi.
Vi who?
Vi not?!

Knock–knock.

Who's there?
Vi.
Vi who?
"Vi do fools fall in love?"

Knock–knock.

Who's there?
Vienna.
Vienna who?
Zis is Vienna the section.

Knock–knock.

Who's there?
Vicious.
Vicious who?
Best Vicious!

Knock–knock.

Who's there?
Vile.
Vile who?
Vile the cat's away, the mice vill play!

Knock–knock.

Who's there?
Vilma.
Vilma who?
Vilma dreams come true?

Knock–knock.

Who's there?
Vilma.
Vilma who?
Vilma frog turn into a prince?

Knock–knock.

Who's there?
Viola.
Viola who?
Viola sudden you don't know me?

Knock–knock.

Who's there?
Violet.
Violet who?
Violet the cat out of the bag?

Knock–knock.

Who's there?
Virtue.
Virtue who?
Virtue get those big,
brown eyes?

Knock–knock.

Who's there?
Virus.
Virus who?
Virus you always
singing stupid songs?

Knock–knock.

Who's there?
Viscount.
(Pronounced V-eye-count)
Viscount who?
Viscount you behave?

Knock–knock.

Who's there?
Voodoo.
Voodoo who?
Voodoo you think you
are, the Wolf Man?

Knock–knock.

Who's there?
Waco (pronounced Wake-o)
and El Paso.

Waco and El Paso who?
If I can stay Waco for the test,
I think El Paso.

Knock–knock.

Who's there?
Waddle.

Waddle who?
Waddle I need to
do to get you to use
your brain?

Knock–knock.

Who's there?
Wadsworth.

Wadsworth who?
Wadsworth it to you if
I go away?

Knock–knock.

Who's there?
Waiter.

Waiter who?
Waiter-ound and
you'll see!

Knock–knock.

Who's there?
Waiter.
Waiter who?
"Waiter till the sun shines, Nellie."

Knock–knock.

Who's there?
Waiver.
Waiver who?
Waiver hands in the air.

Knock–knock.

Who's there?
Wallaby.
Wallaby who?
Wallaby in trouble if I keep
knocking on the door?

Knock–knock.

Who's there?
Walter D.
Walter D. who?
Walter D. Lawn.

Knock–knock.

Who's there?
Wanamaker.
Wanamaker who?
Wanamaker mud pie?

Knock–knock.

Who's there?
Wanda.
Wanda who?
Wanda come out and play?

Knock–knock.

Who's there?
Wanda.
Wanda who?
Wanda these days—Pow!

Knock–knock.

Who's there?
Wanda.
Wanda who?
Wanda tell me the password?
It's cold out here.

Knock–knock.

Who's there?
Wanda Witch.
Wanda Witch who?
Wanda Witch you a Merry Christmas.

Knock–knock.

Who's there?
Warden.
Warden who?
Warden the world
are you up to?

Knock–knock.

Who's there?
Warner.
Warner who?
Warner you coming
out to play?

Knock–knock.

Who's there?
Warren.
Warren who?
I'm Warren out!

Knock–knock.

Who's there?
Warren.
Warren who?
Warren my birthday suit.

Knock–knock.

Who's there?
Warren D.
Warren D. who?
Warren D. world are you?

Knock–knock.

Who's there?
Warrior.
   Warrior who?
Warrior been all my life?

Knock–knock.

Who's there?
Warsaw.
   Warsaw who?
Warsaw knock-knock joke
I ever heard.

Knock–knock.

Who's there?
Wash out.
   Wash out who?
Wash out, I'm coming in!

Knock–knock.

Who's there?
Wash.
   Wash who?
Wash you there, Charlie?

Knock–knock.

Who's there?
Water.
Water who?
Water be ashamed of yourself
for living in a dump like this!

Knock–knock.

Who's there?
Water.
Water who?
Water friends for?

Knock–knock.

Who's there?
Watts.
Watts who?
Watts up, Doc?

Knock–knock.

Who's there?
Wayne.
Wayne who?
I'm Wayne D. Outfield.

Knock–knock.

Who's there?
Weasel.
Weasel who?
"Weasel while you work . . ."

Knock–knock.

Who's there?
Weevil.
Weevil who?
Weevil meet again.

Knock–knock.

Who's there?
Wednesday.

Wednesday who?
"Wednesday saints go
marching in . . ."

Knock–knock.

Who's there?
Weirdo.

Weirdo who?
Weirdo you think
you're going?

Knock–knock.

Who's there?
Welcome.

Welcome who?
Welcome up and see
me sometime.

Knock–knock.

Who's there?
Wendy.

Wendy who?
"Wendy wind blows,
the cradle will rock . . ."

Knock–knock.

Who's there?
Wendy Katz.

Wendy Katz who?
Wendy Katz away, the mice
will play.

Knock–knock.

Who's there?
Werner.

Werner who?
Werner you going
to grow up?

Knock–knock.

Who's there?
West Point.
West Point who?
West Point are you trying to make?

Knock–knock.

Who's there?
Wheelbarrow.
Wheelbarrow who?
Wheelbarrow some money
and go on a trip.

Knock–knock.

Who's there?
Whelan.
Whelan who?
That's all Whelan good, but I still
think you're a nut.

Knock–knock.

Who's there?
Whitmore.
Whitmore who?
Whitmore can I say after I say I'm sorry?

Knock–knock.

Who's there?
Whitney.
Whitney who?
Whitney have to say to me?

Knock–knock.

Who's there?
Whittier.

Whittier who?
Whittier think my chances are
for getting inside?

Knock–knock.

Who's there?
Who.

Who who?
Terrible echo in here, isn't there?

Knock–knock.

Who's there?
Widow.

Widow who?
A widow kid.

Knock–knock.

Who's there?
Wiener.

Wiener who?
Wiener takes all.

Knock–knock.

Who's there?
Will F.
Will F. who?
Will F. Iron.

Knock–knock.

Who's there?
Willard.
Willard who?
Willard be too late if I
come back in an hour?

Knock–knock.

Who's there?
William Tell.
William Tell who?
William Tell your mommy to
come to the door?

Knock–knock.

Who's there?
Willoughby.
Willoughby who?
Willoughby my Valentine?

Knock–knock.

Who's there?
Willie.
Willie who?
Willie or won't he?

Knock–knock.

Who's there?
Wilson.
Wilson who?
Wilson body let me in?

Knock–knock.

Who's there?
Winnie.
Winnie who?
Winnie you going to
open the door?

Knock–knock.

Who's there?
Winott.
Winott who?
Winott leave your brain to
science? Maybe they can find
a cure for it.

HEE
HEE

Knock–knock.

Who's there?
Wolf.
Wolf who?
Wolf-er goodness sake, Grandma,
what big teeth you have!

Knock–knock.

Who's there?
Wire.
Wire who?
Wire we telling knock-knock jokes?

Knock–knock.

Who's there?
Wooden.
Wooden who?
Wooden you like to know!

Knock–knock.

Who's there?
Wienie.
Wienie who?
Wienie more jokes like these!

Knock–knock.

Who's there?
Archibald.
Archibald who?
Archibald real tears when he
read these knock-knock jokes.

Knock–knock.

Who's there?
Wok.
Wok who?
Wok, don't run.

Knock–knock.

Who's there?
Woody.
Woody who?
Woody lady of the house
please open the door?

Knock–knock.

Who's there?
Woody.
Woody who?
Woody you care who this is?

Knock–knock.

Who's there?
Woolly.
Woolly who?
Woolly win the race?

Knock–knock.

Who's there?
Woody.
Woody who?
Woody want me to say?

HA!

Knock–knock.

Who's there?
Wyatt.
Wyatt who?
Wyatt always pours when it rains?

Knock–knock.

Who's there?
Wyatt.
Wyatt who?
Wyatt the world do I
bother to talk to you?

Knock–knock.

Who's there?
Wyden.
Wyden who?
Wyden you tell me
you were a werewolf?

Knock–knock.

Who's there?
Wynn.
Wynn who?
Wynn a few—lose a few.

Knock–knock.

Who's there?

X.

X who?

X (Eggs) Benedict!

Knock–knock.

Who's there?

X.

X who?

X (Eggs) for breakfast.

Knock–knock.

Who's there?

Xavier.

Xavier who?

Xavier breath!

I'm not leaving.

Knock–knock.

Who's there?

Xavier.

Xavier who?

Xavier self!

Knock–knock.

Who's there?
Xena.
Xena who?
Xena picture in the paper.

Knock–knock.

Who's there?
Xenia.
Xenia who?
Xenia open the door
last week!

Knock–knock.

Who's there?
Oh Mama!
Oh Mama who?
Oh Mama-stake
(oh, my mistake)!

Knock–knock.

Who's there?
Xenia.
Xenia who?
Xenia stealing my magazine.

Knock–knock.

Who's there?
Yale.

Yale who?
"Yale, Caesar."

Knock–knock.

Who's there?
Yates.

Yates who?
Crazy Yates (Eights)!

Knock–knock.

Who's there?
Yawl.

Yawl who?
Yawl come back, you hear.

Knock–knock.

Who's there?
Yeti.

Yeti who?
Yeti-nother knock-knock joke!

Knock–knock.

Who's there?
Yoda.
Yoda who?
Yoda smart one, you tell me.

Knock–knock.

Who's there?
Yoga.
Yoga who?
Yoga your way, I'll go mine.

Knock–knock.

Who's there?
Yogurt.
Yogurt who?
Yogurt to be joking!

Knock–knock.

Who's there?
Arno.
Arno who?
Arno you don't!

Knock–knock.

Who's there?
Yoko.
Yoko who?
Yoko jump in the lake.

Knock–knock.

Who's there?
Yokohama.
Yokohama who?
Yokohama (you can have my)
place in line!

Knock–knock.

Who's there?
Yokum.
Yokum who?
"Yokum a long way, baby . . ."

Knock–knock.

Who's there?
Your sister.
Your sister who?
You mean you don't know me?

Knock–knock.

Who's there?
Yucatan.
Yucatan who?
Yucatan dollars to pay the taxi?

Knock–knock.

Who's there?
Yolette.
Yolette who?
Would Yolette me in the door,
please?

Knock–knock.

Who's there?
Wilma.
Wilma who?
Wilma jokes make you open the door?

Knock–knock.

Who's there?
Ozzie.
Ozzie who?
Ozzie (I see) I'm going to be
out here all night.

Knock–knock.

Who's there?
Yukon.
Yukon who?
Yukon say that again!

Knock–knock.

Who's there?
Yucca.

Yucca who?
Yucca be arrested for impersonating a human being.

Knock–knock.

Who's there?
Yukon.

Yukon who?
Yukon win 'em all.

Knock–knock.

Who's there?
Yukon.

Yukon who?
Yukon (you can't) teach an old dog new tricks!

Knock–knock.

Who's there?
Yul.

Yul who?
Yul look wonderful.
Who is your embalmer?

Knock–knock.

Who's there?
Yule.

Yule who?
Yule never guess.

Knock–knock.

Who's there?
Yuma.
Yuma who?
The Good Yuma man.

Knock–knock.

Who's there?
Yuri.
Yuri who?
Yuri mind me of the Liberty
Bell—half-cracked.

Knock–knock.

Who's there?
Zachery.
Zachery who?
Zachery what I want for Christmas.

Knock–knock.

Who's there?
Zany.
Zany who?
Zany body out there?!

Knock–knock.

Who's there?
Zeal.
Zeal who?
Zeal it with a kiss.

Knock–knock.

Who's there?
Zelda.
Zelda who?
Zelda family jewels!

Knock–knock.

Who's there?
Zenka.
Zenka who?
Zenka you for your kind words.

Knock–knock.

Who's there?
Zest.
Zest who?
Zest things in life are free.

Knock–knock.

Who's there?
Zinc.
Zinc who?
Zinc or swim!

Knock–knock.

Who's there?
Zinc.
Zinc who?
Zinc of you all the time!

Knock–knock.

Who's there?
Zinnia.
Zinnia who?
There's method Zinnia madness.

Knock–knock.

Who's there?
Zipper and Zipper.
Zipper and Zipper who?
"Zipper D. Doodah and Zipper D. A. . . ."

Knock–knock.

Who's there?
Zits.
Zits who?
Zits down and concentrate.

Knock–knock.

Who's there?
Zoe.
Zoe who?
Zoe (so we) meet again!

Knock–knock.

Who's there?
Zone.
Zone who?
Zone worst enemy.

Knock–knock.

Who's there?
Zoo.
Zoo who?
Zoo long for now!

Knock–knock.

Who's there?
Cy.
Cy who?
Cy O'Nara (Sayonara)!

Knock–knock.

Who's there?
Zoophyte.
Zoophyte who?
Zoophyte anyone who bothers the animals.

Knock–knock.

Who's there?
Zuccarelli.
Zuccarelli who?
Zuccarelli long time to get to
the last knock-knock joke!

Knock–knock.

Who's there?
Zymosis.
Zymosis who?
Zymosis come back with the Ten Commandments?

TONGUE TWISTERS

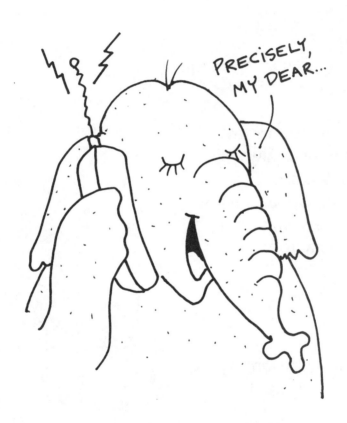

Ape cakes, grape cakes.
Ape cakes, grape cakes.
Ape cakes, grape cakes.

Andrea and Andrew ate
eight acid apples accidentally.

Angus' angry answer annoyed
Angie's aunt. Angus is always
annoying Angie's aunt.
Angus actually enjoys annoying
Angie's aunt. It's awful, although
Angie's aunt only acts annoyed.

If I assist a sister-assistant, will
the sister's sister-assistant
assist me?

"What ails Alex?" asks Alice.

The little addled
adder added ads.

Abbie's Aunt Annie isn't
answering Abbie's Aunt Amy.

Ada made a 'gator hate her, so the 'gator ate her.

All artists aren't artful.
There are artful artists and awful artists.
Although there are a lot of awesome artful artists,
annoying awful artists occur more often.

Angels hang ancient anchors at angles that anger ogres.

Arnie's oranges aren't as orange as Arnold's oranges.

Are there auks in the Arctic or aren't there auks in the Arctic? And if there are auks in the Arctic, are they auctioning arks?

SEEN ANY AUKS?

Ava ate eighty eggs.
Ava ate eighty eggs.
Ava ate eighty eggs.

Abe and Babe will grab a grub from Greg.
Will Abe and Babe grab a grub from Greg?
If Abe and Babe will grab a grub from Greg, where's the grub from Greg Abe and Babe will grab?

Al's ally is in the alley.

All Al's sly allies lie.

Adele is a dull adult.

Aunt Edith's anteater ate Aunt Edith's ants.

Eight apes ate Nate's tape.

Never ever offer awful
Arthur alfalfa.

Ann Anteater ate Andy
Alligator's apples, so angry
Andy Alligator ate
Ann Anteater's ants.

Adam ate an autumn
apple.

Ancient anchors anchor
ancient arks.

Can an active actor always actually act accurately?

Are Archie and Audrey's
archery arrows as arty as
Artie's archery arrows?

Alice asks for axes.
Alice asks for axes.
Alice asks for axes.

A man demanded Amanda's panda.

Ashley's leaping as she's sleeping.

Avery's army's armory.
Avery's army's armory.
Avery's army's armory.

Big boxes of bears being brought aboard.

Rubber baby-buggy bumpers.
Rubber baby-buggy bumpers.
Rubber baby-buggy bumpers.

Once upon a barren moor
There dwelt a bear; also a boar.
The bear could not bear the boar,
The bear thought the boar a bore.
At last the bear could bear no more
That boar that bored him on the moor.
And so one morn he bored the boar—
that boar will bore no more!

HEE
HEE

Beware! That's a bear lair. I wouldn't go in there on a dare. In there is where a bear scared Pierre. Pierre was not aware of the bear in the lair until the bear gave a glare and Pierre ran from there.

A big bug hit a bold bald bear and the bold bald bear bled blood badly.

Who bit the bold bald bear on the shoulder on the boulder and made the bold bald bear on the boulder bawl?

Brandy bandaged the bear.

Bobby Bear's B-B bean shooter.
Bobby Bear's B-B bean shooter.
Bobby Bear's B-B bean shooter.

The big bloke bled in the big blue bed.

Brenda Black was blameless.

Betty better butter Buddy's brother's bagel. But before Betty butters the bagel, Betty better boil and bake the bagel.

Bruce brought big biscuits.
Bob brought both briskets.

A box of biscuits, a box of mixed biscuits, and a biscuit mixer.

Blake the baker bakes black bread.

The bottom of the butter bucket is the buttered bucket bottom.

Menu

Bad black bran bread.
Bad black bran bread.
Bad black bran bread.

"The bun is better buttered," Buffy muttered.

Bring the brown baked bread back.

Brian's bride bakes buns, but Brian buys baked bread.

Aiken Bacon was baking bacon.
The bacon he was bakin' was bought in Macon. So he was makin' baked Macon bacon.

Bill blows big blimpy bubbles.
When Bill's big, blimpy bubbles burst,
Bill began to blubber.
Bill was a big blimpy baby.

Betty Block blows big black bubbles.

A bachelor botched a batch of badly baked biscuits.
Did the bachelor botch a batch of badly baked biscuits?
If the bachelor botched a batch of badly baked biscuits,
Where are the badly baked biscuits the bachelor botched?

Betty Botter bought a bit of butter.
"But," said she, "this butter's bitter.
If I put it in my batter, it will make my batter bitter.
But a bit of better butter—
That would make my batter better."
So Betty Botter bought a
bit of better butter (better than her bitter butter) and made her
bitter batter a bit better.

I bought a bit of baking powder and baked a batch of biscuits. I brought a big basket of biscuits back to the bakery and baked a basket of big biscuits. Then I took the big basket of biscuits and the basket of big biscuits and mixed the big biscuits with the basket of biscuits that was next to the big basket and put a bunch of biscuits from the basket into a biscuit mixer and brought the basket of biscuits and the box of mixed biscuits and the biscuit mixer to the bakery—and opened a can of sardines.

Byron's butler bought Byron's brother butter.

Bess's pet pestered Fess.
Bess's pet pestered Fess.
Bess's pet pestered Fess.

Bernie's thirty dirty turtles dirtied Ernie.

Bennie bought a bright brown
blouse for Bonnie, but Bonnie
believed Bennie bought a
better bright blue blouse for Betty.

Big pigs in a big pig pen.

Brownie Birdie was a bully.
Brownie's bossy brother Billy
Birdie was a bigger bully.
Brownie and Billy stayed
busy by bullying their buddies. Both
Birdie brothers were big, bad bullies.

Brown, black, blue.

Bill built a big brick building.
Bill built a big brick building.
Bill built a big brick building.

Bridget builds bigger bridges than Barbara, but the bridges Barbara builds are better than the bridges Bridget builds.

The fuzzy bee buzzed the buzzy busy beehive.

The bumblebees' buzzing didn't bother the beavers nor did the beavers' building bother the bumblebees.

Bruce's bird is perched on the broken birch branch.

Bluebirds in blue birdbaths.

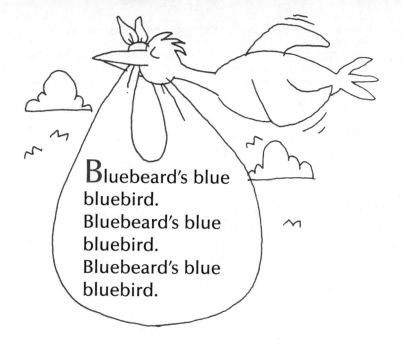

Bluebeard's blue
bluebird.
Bluebeard's blue
bluebird.
Bluebeard's blue
bluebird.

A batter, a banana, and a bandanna.
A batter, a banana, and a bandanna.
A batter, a banana, and a bandanna.

Both bowlers bought blue bowling balls, but both bowled
better with black bowling balls.

Bulb-bowls.
Bulb-bowls.
Bulb-bowls.

The bleak breeze blights the brightly blooming blossom.
Bright bloom the blossoms on the brook's bare brown banks.

Bob's blue blobs.
Bob's blue blobs.
Bob's blue blobs.

Blue beads in a blue rattle rattle blue beads.

Biff Brown bluffed and blustered.

Brad brought Barney's bright brass bike back.

Buster broke broncos. Buster was a bronco buster.

YEE-HAW!

"Did you bust the butcher's buzzer, Buster?"
"You bet I busted the buzzer," Buster boasted.

I'll bet Beth's beau Brett brought Beth both bikes.

The bootblack brought the black boot back.

Blair's blue boots are beauties.

A big blue bucket of blue blackberries.

Billy's big black-and-blue blister bled.

Biff Brown split bricks.

The best breath test tests breath better.

Blake broke both black bricks, but brought both brown bricks Britt borrowed.

Red bug's blood, bed bug's blood.
Red bug's blood, bed bug's blood.
Red bug's blood, bed bug's blood.

I have a black-backed bath brush.
Do you have a black-backed bath brush?

Black bug's blood.
Black bug's blood.
Black bug's blood.

Beth bathed in both baths.

Pass the big black blank bank book. If you won't pass the big black blank bank book back, then pass the small brown blank bank book back.

Bland Bea blinks back.
Bland Bea blinks back.
Bland Bea blinks back.

The brave bloke blocked the broken back bank door.

The boy blinked at the blank bank blackboard.

Bill had a billboard.
Bill also had a board bill.
The board bill bored Bill,
So Bill sold his billboard
And paid his board bill.
Then the board bill
No longer bored Bill,
But though he had no board bill,
Neither did he have his billboard.

Betty's betting big.

Three blind mice blew bugles.

Bring Beverly a bubbling, bubbling beverage.

Borrowed burros bring borrowed barrels.

Bertha blocked the bleached back beach benches.

Bob bought a bleached blue-beaded blazer.

Bess is the best backward blue-blowing bugler in the Boston brass band.

The blunt back blade is bad.

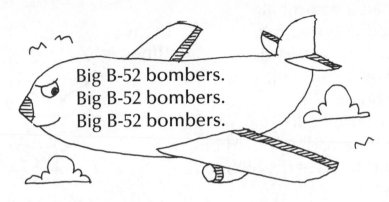

Big B-52 bombers.
Big B-52 bombers.
Big B-52 bombers.

Ted Blake's back brake-block broke a bearing.
Did Ted Blake's back brake-block break a bearing?
If Ted Blake's back brake-block broke a bearing,
Where's the bearing Ted Blake's back brake-block broke?

A big black bat flew past.
A big brown bat flew past.
Did the big black bat fly past faster than
the big brown bat flew past?

A bitter biting bittern
Bit a better brother bittern,
And the better bittern bit the bitter biter back.
And the bittern, bitten
By the better biting bittern,
Said, "I'm a bitten, bitter, biting, bittern, bitten better now, alack!"

Bad bumblebee boo-boo.
Bad bumblebee boo-boo.
Bad bumblebee boo-boo.

Baked beans bring bad dreams.
Baked beans bring bad dreams.
Baked beans bring bad dreams.

Barbara's brother's baking brown bread.
Barbara's brother's baking brown bread.
Barbara's brother's baking brown bread.

Bright blue buggies.
Bright blue buggies.
Bright blue buggies.

Bored boars, busy boars.
Bored boars, busy boars.
Bored boars, busy boars.

Bumble bees boast bumpy knees.
Bumble bees boast bumpy knees.
Bumble bees boast bumpy knees.

Clean clams crammed in clean cans.

Cheap sausage stew.

A canner exceedingly canny,
One morning remarked to his granny,
"A canner can can
Anything that he can,
But a canner can't can a can, can he?"

Catch a can canner canning a can as he does the cancan, and you've caught a can-canning can-canning can canner!

Cuthbert's cufflinks.
Cuthbert's cufflinks.
Cuthbert's cufflinks.

A chapped chap chopped chips.

A cheeky chimp chucked cheap chocolate chips in the cheap chocolate chip shop.

The fish-and-chip shop's chips are soft chips.

Does this shop stock cheap checkers?

Where can I find a cheerful cheap chop suey shop?

Top chopstick shops stock top chopsticks.

Cheerful Charlie chose a cheesy chowder.
Did cheerful Charlie choose a cheesy chowder?
If cheerful Charlie chose a cheesy chowder,
How cheerful was Charlie after he chose the cheesy chowder?

Chris criss-crossed the pie crust.

Caleb grabbed clicking crab claws.

Choice chilled cherries cheer Cheryl.

Clarence claims clams can't clap.

Tricky crickets.
Tricky crickets.
Tricky crickets.

Aunt Connie could'a caught an anaconda, but the anaconda caught Aunt Connie.
Had the anaconda been the kind of anaconda that was kinder, that anaconda could'a kissed Aunt Connie.
But the anaconda that caught Aunt Connie was the kind of anaconda that couldn't kiss, so it consumed Aunt Connie.

Crisp crust crackles.
Crisp crust crackles.
Crisp crust crackles.

A cupcake cook in a cupcake cook's cap cooks cupcakes.

The cute cookie cutters cut cute cookies.
Did the cute cookie cutters cut cute cookies?
If the cute cookie cutters cut cuter cookies,
Where are the cute cookies the cute cookie cutter cut?

Clyde Crow cries quietly.

Crisp cracker crumbs.

Corinne quit cooking quiche because she couldn't quite cook quiche correctly.

If Sue chews shoes, should she choose to chew new shoes or old shoes?

All I want is a proper cup of coffee, made in a proper copper coffeepot. You can believe it or not—I want a cup of coffee in a proper coffeepot. Tin coffeepots or iron coffeepots, they're no use to me. If I can't have a proper cup of coffee in a proper copper coffeepot—I'll have a cup of tea!

Cooper cut Culver's copper-colored clover.

Chester shucked the chestnuts and Chuck chucked the shucks.
Did Chester shuck the chestnuts faster than Chuck chucked
the shucks?
Or did Chuck chuck the shucks faster than Chester shucked
the chestnuts?

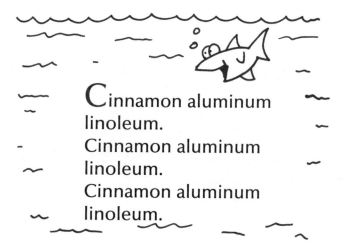

Cinnamon aluminum
linoleum.
Cinnamon aluminum
linoleum.
Cinnamon aluminum
linoleum.

If a good cook could cook cuckoos so fine,
And a good cook could cook cuckoosall the time,
How many cuckoos could a good cook cook
If a good cook could
cook cuckoos?

Choppers chop.
Droppers drop.
Shoppers shop.

NO
WAY!

Carol carefully carried Cora's carrots.

The chief Chief chewed the cheap cheese.

New cheese, blue cheese, chew cheese please.

The class cleaned the cream cheese churners carefully.

Cora Clinger's coolers were cool, but Carla Clinger's coolers were clearly the coolest coolers.

Colin's cooler can't cool Craig's colas.

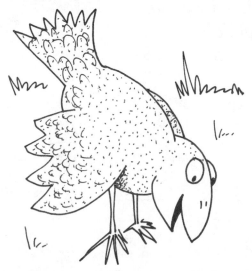

A clan of cool crows clings close in cold climates.

What could have caused the crows to caw?
I think the cars were the cause of the crows' cawing.

Jerry chewed two chewy cherries.

Kookie cookies.
Kookie cookies.
Kookie cookies.

Camels can't keep carpets and closets clean.

How much caramel can a canny cannibal cram in a camel,
if a canny cannibal can cram caramel in a camel?

Clara Kaufman carefully cleaned the carpet in her cousin's kids' clothes closet.

Chloe couldn't close the clothes closet 'cause her clothes were crammed too close.

Clyde can clean Chloe's clothes, but can Clyde cram Chloe's clothes into Chloe's closet?

Carmen is mad at Matt because she paid Matt money to clean her muddy car mats. Matt cleaned Carmen's muddy car and left Carmen's car mats muddy. "Clean the muddy car mats, Matt, not the muddy car," Carmen muttered.

Carol quarreled.
Carol quarreled.
Carol quarreled.

The cop was in the cot copping a catnap. When the cop caught the cat in the cot copping a catnap, the cop kicked the cat-napping cat out of the cot.

The chap in the cap clapped when he captured the cat in the trap.

Clinton's kittens kicked Clinton's chickens. Clinton caught the kicking kittens in the kitchen.
"Quit kicking those chickens, you crazy kicking kittens," Clinton commanded.

Charlene keeps the chalk sharp. As she sharpens the chalk, the chalk gets short. So she keeps a "sharp chalk chart" to show when to change the chalk.

Carl called Claude.
Carl called Claude.
Carl called Claude.

Ann Chan can't chant.
Chancey's aunt's chants.

Had the colt had a coat, the colt couldn't have caught cold.

The cowardly cowboy cowered as the courageous cowboy cornered the cows.

Carl chose Claire's church chimes carefully.

The commander commanded the commandoes.
The commander commanded the commandoes.
The commander commanded the commandoes.

Chip's ship sank.
Chip's ship sank.
Chip's ship sank.

Chris' craft crashed.

A curious cream-colored cat crept into the crypt and crept out again.
Did the curious cream-colored cat creep into the crypt and creep out again?
If the curious cream-colored cat crept into the crypt and crept out again,
Where's the curious cream-colored cat that crept into the crypt and crept out again?

Who checked the chart of the cud-chewing cow?

If you must cross a coarse cross cow across a crowded cow crossing, cross the cross coarse cow across the crowded cow crossing carefully.

A clipper shipped several clipped sheep.
Were these clipped sheep the clipper ship's sheep?
Or just clipped sheep shipped on a clipper ship?

Cheap sheep soup.
Cheap sheep soup.
Cheap sheep soup.

Charles chose the chief cheap sheep section.

"Cheep-cheep," chirped the cheery chick.

A clean, covered coffee cup cupboard.

As I was dashing down Cutting Hill,
A-cutting through the air,
I saw Charlie Cutting sitting
In Oscar Cutting's chair.
And Oscar Cutting was sitting
cutting Charlie Cutting's hair.

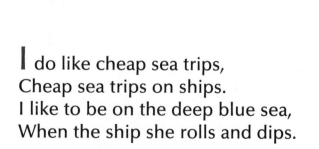

Great crates create great craters, but great craters create greater craters.

I do like cheap sea trips,
Cheap sea trips on ships.
I like to be on the deep blue sea,
When the ship she rolls and dips.

If you cross a cross across a cross,
Or cross a stick across a stick,
Or cross a stick across a cross,
Or cross a cross across a stick,
Or stick a stick across a stick,
Or stick a cross across a cross,
Or stick a cross across a stick,
Or stick a stick across a cross,
What a waste of time!

When the computer crashed, the class gasped.

The creek creatures croaked quietly.

Can Claire cue Carl's curtain call?

A cricket critic cricked his neck at a critical cricket match.

Curt carved curves.
Curt carved curves.
Curt carved curves.

The chicken checkers ought to check the chickens that the chicken catchers caught.

The captain's cook was a crook 'cause he took the clock locked in the captain's kitchen cupboard.

I would if I could,
If I couldn't, how could I?
I couldn't if I couldn't, could I?
Could you if you couldn't,
could you?

Chuck's job was to chop chips. Chuck was a chip chopper.
In fact, he was the top chip chopper.
The chips were shipped to the chip-chopping shop and Chuck chopped the chips.
The chip-chopping shop also had a chip checker.
He checked the chips Chuck chopped.

Cat coats can't keep cats calm.
Cat coats can't keep cats calm.
Cat coats can't keep cats calm.

Cathy coughed coffee on Connie's copy.
Cathy coughed coffee on Connie's copy.
Cathy coughed coffee on Connie's copy.

Clattering across the crooked cobblestones, the hobbled filly faltered home!
Clattering across the crooked cobblestones, the hobbled filly faltered home!
Clattering across the crooked cobblestones, the hobbled filly faltered home!

Cock a doodle do you do, cockatoo to meet you too!
Cock a doodle do you do, cockatoo to meet you too!
Cock a doodle do you do, cockatoo to meet you too!

A cockatoo can keep a tune.
Can tuna fish too swoon the moon?

Coffins often carry off the carrion of chaps who coughed.
Coffins often carry off the carrion of chaps who coughed.
Coffins often carry off the carrion of chaps who coughed.

Come here, complex chameleon!
Come here, complex chameleon!
Come here, complex chameleon!

Could a barracuda cut a can of buttered beans?
Could a barracuda cut a can of buttered beans?
Could a barracuda cut a can of buttered beans?

The cow cried moo, but the crow cawed true.
The cow cried moo, but the crow cawed true.
The cow cried moo, but the crow cawed true.

Crooked crickets kill crops.
Crooked crickets kill crops.
Crooked crickets kill crops.

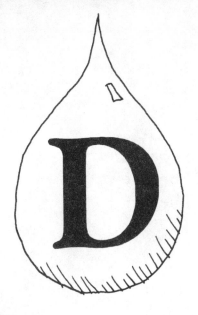

Do drop in at the Dewdrop Inn

How much dew could a dewdrop drop if a dewdrop did drop dew?

My dame had a lame, tame crane;
My dame had a lame, tame crane.
Oh, pray, gentle Jane,
Let my dame's lame crane
Pray drink and come home again.

Dwayne dwells in drafty dwellings.

Does a double bubble gum double bubble?

The duke dropped the dirty double damask dinner napkin.

Down the deep damp dark dank den.

The deer dined on dough, though the doe dined on dates.

Deer's ears hear clear cheers.

A maid with a duster made a furious bluster dusting a bust in the hall. When the bust it was dusted, the bust it was busted, the bust it was dust, that's all.

Debbie didn't destroy Darrell's dishes. Darrell destroyed Debbie's dishes.

Disgruntled dishwashers don't wash dishes.

Jane's drainboard drain just drained Jane's drainage.

Ducks clucked under the docks.

Drew drew dumb ducks drumming drums.

Ducks don't dunk doughnuts.

Dave's dogs dig deep ditches.

Don't you dare dawdle, Darryl!
Don't you dare dawdle, Darryl!
Don't you dare dawdle, Darryl!

Drew dripped the drink from the dipper, but he didn't drink a drop.

When a doctor gets sick and another doctor doctors him, does the doctor doing the doctoring have to doctor the doctor the way the doctor being doctored wants to be doctored, or does the doctor doing the doctoring of the doctor doctor the doctor as he wants to do the doctoring?

Donna didn't date Darla's daddy's dentists, but Darla did.

A dozen dim ding-dongs.
A dozen dim ding-dongs.
A dozen dim ding-dongs.

The detective effectively detected the defective device.

The drummers drummed and the strummers strummed.
The drummers drummed and the strummers strummed.
The drummers drummed and the strummers strummed.

Dave's date dared Dave and Dale to dive. Dave didn't dive. "Darn it, Dale, dive!" Dave's date demanded. "Don't dare Dale," Dave declared. "Dale doesn't do dives."

Dan's little delivery to the livery was delayed.

Darby destroyed Dunby's derby.

The dwarf's dwellings are by the dark wharf. There are dogs by the dark wharf and they woof at the dwarfs as the dwarfs walk on the wharf. When the dark wharf is foggy, the dwarf's dwellings seem far away and that makes the dwarfs wary. That's when the dwarfs wish the dogs on the dark wharf would woof, so the dwarves could weave their way through the fog to their dwellings.
"What are dogs for if not to woof?" the dwarfs wonder.

Dan can't Can-Can, can Don?
Dan can't Can-Can, can Don?
Dan can't Can-Can, can Don?

Don's dad didn't doubt Don didn't do the deed he said he didn't do; he doubted Don didn't do another deed Don did.

Drivel, dribble, quibble, spittle.
Drivel, dribble, quibble, spittle.
Drivel, dribble, quibble, spittle.

Elegant elephants.
Elegant elephants.
Elegant elephants.

Edgar at eight ate eight eggs a day.

Eddie's enemies envied Eddie's energy.

Esau Wood would saw wood. Oh, the wood that Wood would saw! One day Esau Wood saw a saw saw wood as no other wood-saw Wood ever saw would saw wood. Of all the wood-saws Wood ever saw saw wood, Wood never saw a wood-saw that would saw like the wood-saw Wood saw would.
Now Esau saws wood with that wood-saw he saw saw wood.

I saw Esau kissing Kate.
Fact is, we all three saw.
I saw Esau, he saw me,
And she saw I saw Esau.

Did you ever iver ever in your leaf loaf life see the deevil divil devil kiss his weef wofe wife?
No, I neever niver never in my leaf loaf life saw the deevil divil devil kiss his weef wofe wife.

Ere her ear hears her err, her ears err here.

Every errant arrow isn't Aaron's errant arrow.

Ernie yearned to learn to turn urns.

Everett never severed Neville's level.

Exercise instructors instruct struggling exercisers to exercise strongly.

Eloquent elephants telephoned other eloquent elephants.

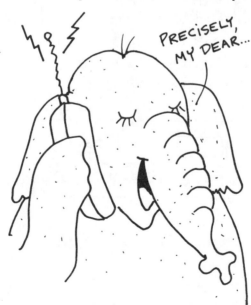

Eleven little leather loafers.
Eleven little leather loafers.
Eleven little leather loafers.

Etta taught her daughter that
she ought to barter smarter.

Eight eager eagles ogled
old Edgar.

Eighteen apes ate
eighteen apricots.
Eighteen apes ate
eighteen apricots.
Eighteen apes ate
eighteen apricots.

Every errand Randy ran for Erin was in error.

For fine fresh fish, phone Phil.

Frank feasted on flaming fish at the famous Friday fish fry.

Free kiwis.
Free kiwis.
Free kiwis.

Can a flying fish flee far from a free fish fry?

Flat, flying fish fly faster than flat, flying fleas.

Fifteen filthy flying foxes.
Fifteen filthy flying foxes.
Fifteen filthy flying foxes.

A fine field of wheat.
A fine field of wheat.
A fine field of wheat.

A fish-sauce shop's sure to sell fresh fish sauce.

The factory fractured the fragile flask.

Flawless porcelain flasks.
Flawless porcelain flasks.
Flawless porcelain flasks.

Fran feeds fish fresh fish food.

The fleas fled far from the ferret's fur.

Fried fresh fish,
Fish fried fresh,
Fresh fried fish.
Fresh fish fried
Or fish fresh fried

A fly and a flea in a flue
Were imprisoned, so what could they do?
Said the fly, "Let us flee!" "Let us fly!" said the flea
And they flew through the flaw in the flue.
Said the flea to the fly as he flew through the flue,
"There's a flaw in the floor of the flue."
Said the fly to the flea as he flew through the flue,
"A flaw in the flue doesn't bother me.
Does it bother you?"

Friendly Bugs

Friendly fleas and fireflies.
Friendly fleas and fireflies.
Friendly fleas and fireflies.

Friendly fleas and huffy fruit flies.
Friendly fleas and huffy fruit flies.
Friendly fleas and huffy fruit flies.

Five fat French fleas freeze.
Five fat French fleas freeze.
Five fat French fleas freeze.

The fruit fly flew through the flute and into the throat of the frightened flutist.

The furry fly flitted from flower to flower.
The furry fly flitted from flower to flower.
The furry fly flitted from flower to flower.

Four fliers flip-flop.
Four fliers flip-flop.
Four fliers flip-flop.

The fickle finger of fate flips fat frogs flat.
The fickle finger of fate flips fat frogs flat.
The fickle finger of fate flips fat frogs flat.

For French shrimp, try a French shrimp shop.

Freddie's frying five fresh flying fish.

Fresh figs.
Fresh figs.
Fresh figs.

Fat flat frozen flounders.
Fat flat frozen flounders.
Fat flat frozen flounders.

Frank freed Fred's fast frog.

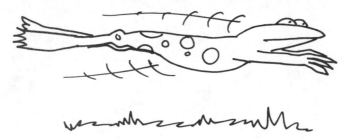

Four fat, flat-footed frogs flapped their floppy flippers.

Five frantic frogs fled from fifty fierce fishes.

Five fifers free,
Fifing in the fog,
Phyllis, Fran,
And Phil and Dan
And Philip's funny frog.

Flighty Flo Fisk and frisky
Fritz Fisk.

Of all the felt I ever felt
I never felt a piece of felt
That felt the same as that felt felt
When I first felt that felt.

Fine fresh fodder.
Fine fresh fodder.
Fine fresh fodder.

A fat-free fruit float.
A fat-free fruit float.
A fat-free fruit float.

Five flashy flappers
Flitting forth fleetly
Found four flighty flappers
Flirting flippantly.

Few free fruit flies fly
from flames.

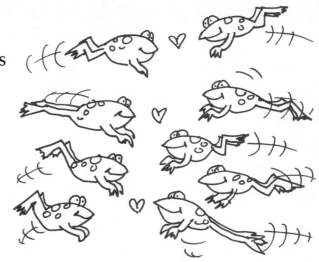

Free flag.
Free flag.
Free flag.

Fifty-five flags
freely flutter
from the floating frigate.

Five flags flying from
A flimsy flagpole.

Three fluffy feathers fell from Phoebe's flimsy fan.

The flood flooded Frank's floor.

Four free-flow pipes flow freely.

Freckle-faced Freddie fidgets.

I'd rather lather Father
Than Father lather me.
When Father lathers
He lathers rather free.

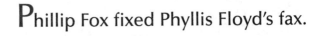

Phillip Fox fixed Phyllis Floyd's fax.

Frisk Fisk first!
Frisk Fisk first!
Frisk Fisk first!

A fly fled fat Flo's flat.
A flea fled fat Flo's flat.
Did the fly or the flea
flee fat Flo's flat first?

Fleming frowned when Fletcher
flung his favorite fossil.

Phil fell four floors face first.

Frank's friend fainted.

Frank faxed the facts in the file folder to his friends in Frankfort.

AAAAHHH....

3RD FLOOR

Phil felt funny folding fifty file folders.

Frank flunked French.

OOO-
LA
LA

F

Fifty-five firefighters fried fifty-five french fries.

I fear this flowered floral fabric is flawed.

Feed the flies fly food, Floyd!

Farrah's flannel fabric frequently frays.

A lively young fisher named Fischer fished for fish from the edge of a fissure. A fish with a grin pulled the fisherman in. Now they're fishing the fissure for Fischer.

Fortunately, Frank Frye's father fixed the phones.

Fleas fly from fries.

Fran's favorite flowers finally flourished.

Four frightening flashes.
Four frightening flashes.
Four frightening flashes.

Fancy Nancy didn't fancy doing fancy work.
But Fancy Nancy's fancy auntie did fancy Nancy doing fancy work. So Fancy Nancy did fancy work for Fancy Nancy's fancy auntie.

Famous Philippine fishery.
Famous Philippine fishery.
Famous Philippine fishery.

Find the fifth filthy outlaw!
Find the fifth filthy outlaw!
Find the fifth filthy outlaw!

Flipping frying flapjacks fills Philip's Friday.
Flipping frying flapjacks fills Philip's Friday.
Flipping frying flapjacks fills Philip's Friday.

Can't a fly ball be called a foul by the fellow who finds fouls without the frothing fans finding fault with his finding of the foul?

Flying fish fry.
Flying fish fry.
Flying fish fry.

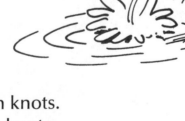

Foxtrots tie feet in knots.
Foxtrots tie feet in knots.
Foxtrots tie feet in knots.

Freaky flies frequently flee French fries.
Freaky flies frequently flee French fries.
Freaky flies frequently flee French fries.

Freely flapping flipper footsteps.
Freely flapping flipper footsteps.
Freely flapping flipper footsteps.

Fresh fish flash fried.
Fresh fish flash fried.
Fresh fish flash fried.

Frilly things fill Phyllis' filmy frock.
Frilly things fill Phyllis' filmy frock.
Frilly things fill Phyllis' filmy frock.

G

Greek grapes.
Greek grapes.
Greek grapes.

The cruel ghoul cooks gruel.

Gargoyles gargle oil.

Granny gave Gary grape gum.

Gus goes by Blue Goose bus.

Granny's gray goose goes last.

Gail grew great grapes.

Great gray geese graze gaily daily.

Goats and ghosts.
Goats and ghosts.
Goats and ghosts.

Gig-whip.
Gig-whip.
Gig-whip.

Good gunsmoke, bad gunsmoke.
Good gunsmoke, bad gunsmoke.
Good gunsmoke, bad gunsmoke.

Cows graze in droves on grass that grows on grooves in groves.

Gale's great glass globe glows green.

The glum groom grew glummer.

Gretchen's guests always get garlic grits. The guests act glad to get the grits, but the guests agree that Gretchen's garlic grits are gross.

Glenda glued Gilda's galoshes.
Glenda glued Gilda's galoshes.
Glenda glued Gilda's galoshes.

Granny Greer greased the gears with green gear grease.

Gophers go golfing.

The grumpy guppy grimly grinned.

Grant grasped at the grass.

Glen lent Gwen Wayne's wrench.

Gene cleans queens' screens.

Glum Gwendolyn's glasses.
Glum Gwendolyn's glasses.
Glum Gwendolyn's glasses.

Three gray-green greedy geese, feeding on a weedy piece.
The piece was weedy, and the geese were greedy, three
gray-green greedy geese.

Glory grows gladioli.
Glory grows gladioli.
Glory grows gladioli.

Higgledy-Piggledy.
Higgledy-Piggledy.
Higgledy-Piggledy.

The hare's ear heard ere the hare heeded.

The hairy hare stares at the hairier hare, and the hairier hare stares at the hairiest hare. Here we have a three-hare stare affair.

PSSSST!

Horrible Heidi hears hairy Horace holler.

Like 'em?

Hugh chooses huge shoes.

Has Hal's heel healed?
Has Hal's heel healed?
Has Hal's heel healed?

Hurry, Harry!
Hurry, Harry!
Hurry, Harry!

Hillary's hairy hound hardly hurries.

How much hair could a hairnet net, if a hairnet could net hair?

Hannah had her hair henna'd.
Hannah had her hair henna'd.
Hannah had her hair henna'd.

Harry Hunt hunts heavy hairy hares.
Does Harry Hunt hunt heavy hairy hares?
If Harry Hunt hunts heavy hairy hares,
Where are the heavy hairy hares Harry Hunt hunts?

Heed the head henpecker!

"Hello, Harry Healy!" hollered Holly Hartley.

If a Hottentot taught
A Hottentot tot,
To talk ere the tot could totter,
Ought the Hottentot tot
Be taught to say "ought,"
Or what ought to be taught her?

Hiccup teacup!
Hiccup teacup!
Hiccup teacup!

If to hoot and to toot
A Hottentot tot
Was taught by a Hottentot tutor,
Should the tutor get hot
If the Hottentot tot
Hoots and toots at the
Hottentot tutor?

Harry helped Herman herd a herd of Herefords.

A hard-hearted shorn honker honked his horned horn hatefully.

Harlan hid from the hornets he heard humming in the hollow hornet tree.

In Huron a hewer, Hugh Hughes, Hewed yews of unusual hues.
Hugh Hughes used blue yews
To build sheds for new ewes;
So his new ewes blue-hued ewe-sheds use.

How hollow Helen Hull hobbles on hills!

Horse hairs are coarse hairs, of course.

A haddock!
A haddock!
A black-spotted haddock!
A black spot
On the black back
Of a black-spotted haddock!

Old Howell owned a house on which old owls howled.

Handsome Hanson ran some mansion, handed down from son to grandson.

Heavy-hearted hippo hugs.
Heavy-hearted hippo hugs.
Heavy-hearted hippo hugs.

Hooper hoped he'd hit a homer, but Hooper hit his hurt hand.
Hooper hoped he'd hit a homer, but Hooper hit his hurt hand.
Hooper hoped he'd hit a homer, but Hooper hit his hurt hand.

Ike ships ice chips in ice chips ships.

Isis envies Isley's ivy.

Can you imagine an imaginary menagerie manager imagining managing an imaginary menagerie?

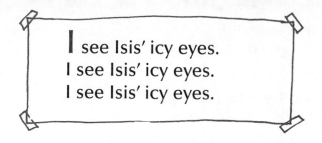

I see Isis' icy eyes.
I see Isis' icy eyes.
I see Isis' icy eyes.

Indianapolis isn't in India, Andy. Indians are in India and Indians are in Indiana. But the Indian Indians and the Indiana Indians aren't identical Indians. The Indians in India are Indian Indians, and the Indians in Indiana are indigenous Indians.

Ira acquired iron awnings.

Insects. Six insects. Six sick insects.

Isn't Isadora adorable?

Iggy is interested in visiting with Izzy, but Izzy isn't interested in visiting with Iggy. Even so, in this instance, Izzy isn't even in, so Izzy couldn't visit with Iggy even if Izzy was interested, which he isn't.

There is pie in my eye.
Will I cry? Will I die?
Though I'm shy, I won't lie.
It might cause a sty, but I deny that I'll die or cry
from the pie in my eye.

Inconsiderate intruders introduce other inconsiderate intruders.

I'll lie idle on the isle.

Our Joe wants to know if your Joe will lend our Joe your Joe's banjo.
If your Joe won't lend our Joe your Joe's banjo, our Joe won't lend your Joe our Joe's banjo when our Joe has a banjo!

Joe's giraffe juggled jelly jars.
Jack's giraffe juggled jam jars.

June sheep sleep soundly.

Are those jesters joking or are those jesters jousting?

Jules the jeweler generally chooses Jewel's jewelry.

James the jailer changed the jail's chairs and chained the chairs to the jail.

A gentle judge judges justly.
A gentle judge judges justly.
A gentle judge judges justly.

James jostled Jean while Jean jostled Joan.

Jim jogs in the gym. Jane jogs in the jungle.

Kinky kite kits.
Kinky kite kits.
Kinky kite kits.

Nutty Knott was not in.
Nutty Knott was out,
Knotting knots in netting.
Nutty Knott was out,
But lots of nots
Were in Nutty Knott's knotty netting.

Come kick six sticks quick.

Keep clean socks in a clean sock stack.

Knee deep, deep knee.
Knee deep, deep knee.
Knee deep, deep knee.

Kirk's starched shirts.

Keenly cleaning copper kettles.
Keenly cleaning copper kettles.
Keenly cleaning copper kettles.

Kiss her quick!
Kiss her quicker!
Kiss her quickest!

King Kong plays Ping-Pong.

Kayaking keeps Katherine's kangaroo calm, but Katherine's kangaroo can't kayak in Kansas, so Katherine carts her kangaroo to Kentucky where her kangaroo can kayak quietly.

A knapsack strap.
A knapsack strap.
A knapsack strap.

This disk sticks.
This disk sticks.
This disk sticks.

The knight's wife knit the knight new knickers.

A lump of red leather.
A red leather lump.

Lily Little lit a little lamp.
Lily Little lit a little lamp.
Lily Little lit a little lamp.

Little Ida lied a little.
Little Ida lied a lot.

Red Leather!
Yellow leather!

Larry's lair lacks locks.

Lonely lowland llamas are ladylike.

Lanky Lawrence lost his lass and lobster.
Did Lanky Lawrence lose his lass and lobster?
If Lanky Lawrence lost his lass and lobster,
Where's the lass and lobster Lanky Lawrence lost?

Lee loves to rob lobsters.

Let lame lambs live.
Let lame lambs live.
Let lame lambs live.

Lizzie's dizzy lizard didn't litter Lizzie's lot.

Local loggers' lawyers.

High roller.
Low roller.
Lower a roller.

Larry sent the latter a letter later.

Literally literary.
Literally literary.
Literally literary.

Lester lists the lesser lesson last.

Lesser leather never weathered lesser wetter weather.

Lemon-lime liniment.
Lemon-lime liniment.
Lemon-lime liniment.

Little licorice lollipops.
Little licorice lollipops.
Little licorice lollipops.

Lisa laughed listlessly.

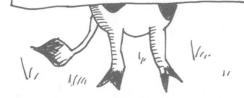

Luke likes licorice.
Luke likes licorice.
Luke likes licorice.

Loose loops.

The less the lame loon
leaned on its little lame leg,
the less the loon limped.

Long lush lashes.

> Luminous aluminum.
> Luminous aluminum.
> Luminous aluminum.

Levi left the leaves lying on the littered lawn.

Lon Longman loaded a lotta long logs.
If Long Longman loaded a lotta long logs,
then where are all the long logs Lon Longman loaded?

Libby locked Larry in the lobby.
"Mom! Libby locked me in the lobby,"
Larry lamented.
"Let Larry loose, Libby,"
Mom laughed.

The llama loaned the lamb a long
ladder.
The lamb loaned the llama a little lamp.

He who laughs last laughs last.

Mummies munch much mush;
Monsters munch much mush;
Many mummies and monsters
Must munch much mush.

Michael's mouse munched
muffins.

MUNCH!

A missing mixture measure.
A missing mixture measure.
A missing mixture measure.

The minx mixed a medicine mixture.

Moses supposes his toeses are roses; but Moses supposes erroneously; for nobody's toeses are poses of roses as Moses supposes his toeses to be.

Mr. Melton made a metal motor.
Mr. Melton made a metal motor.
Mr. Melton made a metal motor.

Mussels with mustard is Mister Mussman's main meal.

Mister Mitter admitted that he missed Mrs. Mitter.

Miss Smith lisps as she talks and lists as she walks.

"Are you aluminiuming, my man?"
"No, I'm copperbottoming 'em, mum."

Mark's name makes Nate's namesake shake.

I miss my Swiss Miss.
My Swiss Miss misses me.

Much mashed mushrooms.
Much mashed mushrooms.
Much mashed mushrooms.

A mermaid made Mike
marmalade.

Matt's mismatched mittens make Matt miserable.

The monster's mother made many morsels for
the monster to munch. Most of the morsels the
monster's mother made were moist, but the
most moist morsels were mainly the morsels
that the monster munched. "My, my," the
monster's mother murmured. "My little
monster may have made a mistake. Too many
moist morsels may make you miserable."

Nick knits Nixon's knickers.

Nellie's new knitting needles
knit neatly.

Nineteen nice knights.
Nineteen nice knights.
Nineteen nice knights.

No one knows Wayne.

I need not your needles,
They're needless to me,
For the needing of needles
Is needless, you see.
But did my neat trousers
But need to be kneed,
I then should have need
Of your needles indeed.

Nine nimble noblemen nibbled nuts.

Nicholas noticed a nick on Nicollette's necklace.

Nippy Noodle nipped his neighbor's nutmegs.
Did Nippy Noddle nip his neighbor's nutmegs?
If Nippy Noodle nipped his neighbor's nutmegs,
Where are the neighbor's nutmegs Nippy Noodle nipped?

Nine nice night nymphs.
Nine nice night nymphs.
Nine nice night nymphs.

Nina never knew her neighbor Noah knew her.

Ned Nott was shot and
Sam Shott was not.
So it's better to be Shott
than Nott.
Some say Nott was not
shot, but Shott swears he
shot Nott.
Either the shot Shott shot at
Nott was not shot, or Nott
was shot.
But if the shot Shott shot
shot Shott himself,
Then Shott would be shot
and Nott would not.
However, the shot Shott shot shot not Shott but Nott.
It's not easy to say who was shot and who was not.
But we know who was Shott and who was Nott.

Norse myths.
Norse myths.
Norse myths.

There's no need to
light a night light on
a light night like
tonight; For a night
light's just a slight
light, on a light night
like tonight.

Nancy naps at noon and Nick knows it's not nice to knock when Nancy's napping.

Knit this net with neat knots. Knots that are not neat are not the knots this net needs.

Ninety-nine knitted knick-knacks were nicked by ninety-nine knitted knick-knack nickers.

"Nighty-night, knight," said one knight to the other knight the other night.
"Ninety night, knight," answered the other knight the other night.

Nine nannies needed new knitting needles nightly, for the knitting needing mending.
Nine nannies needed new knitting needles nightly, for the knitting needing mending.
Nine nannies needed new knitting needles nightly, for the knitting needing mending.

Ninety-nine and ninety-nine added is twice times ninety-nine.

One worm wiggled while
Two tiny toads tasted tea while
Three thirsty turkeys thought while
Four frantic flamingoes flapped while
Five ferocious felines flashed their fangs while
Six slow sloths silently slept while
Seven stinky skunks started singing while
Eight elderly elks eloped while
Nine needlefish knitted napkins while
Ten tarantulas tapped tambourines.

HA!

Old oily corks.

"Under the mother otter," uttered the other otter.

Awful old Ollie oils oily autos.

The owner of the Inside Inn
Was outside his Inside Inn
With his inside outside his Inside Inn.

Oliver Oglethorpe ogled an owl and oyster.
Did Oliver Oglethorpe ogle an owl and oyster?
If Oliver Oglethorpe ogled an owl and oyster,
Where's the owl and oyster Oliver Oglethorpe ogled?

Orville ordered ordinary ornaments.

An oyster met an oyster,
And they were oysters two;
Two oysters met two oysters,
And they were oysters too;
Four oysters met a pint of milk,
And they were oyster stew.

Peter Piper picked a peck of pickled pepper,
A peck of pickled peppers Peter Piper picked.
If Peter Piper picked a peck of pickled peppers,
Where's the peck of pickled peppers Peter Piper picked?

The perky parrot playfully pecked the pirate's pate.

Peck
Peck

The playful purple parrot pecked
the pink parrot's plume.

Pairs of parakeets parent parrots
perfectly.

Pass the pink peas please.

Plain bun, plum bun.
Plain bun, plum bun.
Plain bun, plum bun.

Please prune plum trees promptly.

The plum pickers plucked the plump plums.
The plum pickers plucked the plump plums.
The plum pickers plucked the plump plums.

Pat, please pass Patsy's plum party patties.

A panda playing with paper placed her paw on a piece of parchment and promptly produced a paw print.

Peter Potter splattered a plate of peas on Patty Platt's pink plaid pants.

Phyllis Bickle spilled Bill Spector's sack of speckled pickles.

Penny penned a pretty poem.

Patty probably purchased plenty pretty party paper.

Polly painted a plate of pasta on Peter's pizza parlor poster.

Peter Piper paid for pepperoni pizza.
If Peter Piper paid for pepperoni pizza,
Then where's the pepperoni pizza
Peter Piper purchased?

Peter poked a poker at the piper, so
the piper poked pepper at Peter.

Paul, please pause for proper applause.

A peck of pesky pixies.
A peck of pesky pixies.
A peck of pesky pixies.

Picky pickpockets pick picked pockets.

Pop bottles pop-bottles in pop shops;
The pop-bottles Pop bottles poor Pop drops.
When Pop drops pop-bottles, pop-bottles plop;
When pop-bottles topple, Pop mops slop.

Painters
Planters
Pointers

Please place the pleated pressed pants on the plain pressing plank.

Preshrunk skirts.
Preshrunk skirts.
Preshrunk skirts.

Please, Pam, put proper pleats in Pete's pants.

Pastor Craster can plaster casts faster than the last pastor.

Pat pet Peg's pig.

Peg's parrot pecked Pat, Peg's pets, the pig, and the parrot.

Paul put a pound of pretzels in a purple paper pouch.

Peggy Babcock's mummy.
Peggy Babcock's mummy.
Peggy Babcock's mummy.

Pretty precious plants.

Polly planted potted plants.

Poor pure Pierre.
Poor pure Pierre.
Poor pure Pierre.

Please prepare the paired pared pears near the unprepared pears near the pool.

Pop's popcorn popper probably popped the popcorn properly.

Preston's probably polishing Peter's pretty pewter pots.

People pay pros for playing.

Peter's plane is plainly painted. Peter is paid plenty to paint planes.

Mr. Pletcher paints Mrs. Pitcher pictures of peaches.

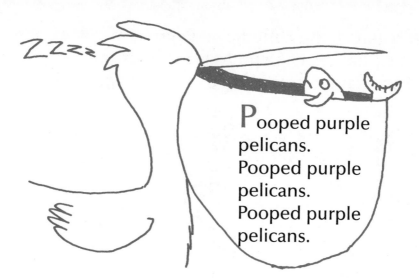

Pooped purple
pelicans.
Pooped purple
pelicans.
Pooped purple
pelicans.

Pick a purple pocket.
Pick a purple pocket.
Pick a purple pocket.

Is a pleasant peasant's pheasant present?

The prince pinched the
princess, so the princess
pinched the prince.

Pale pink plumage.
Pale pink plumage.
Pale pink plumage.

Matt batted, Patty putted, and Pepe punted.
Then Patty batted, Pepe putted, and Matt punted.
Then Pepe batted, Matt putted, and Patty punted.

When platters shatter, scatter.
They splatter matter.

Pretty poor peace prospects.

A park's a perfect place to pace.
A park's a perfect place to pace.
A park's a perfect place to pace.

Peach eating beats peach pitting!
Peach eating beats peach pitting!
Peach eating beats peach pitting!

Perfect your posture in the pasture.
Perfect your posture in the pasture.
Perfect your posture in the pasture.

Perfectly proper princesses prepare pies.
Perfectly proper princesses prepare pies.
Perfectly proper princesses prepare pies.

Peter properly prepares pepper powder.
Peter properly prepares pepper powder.
Peter properly prepares pepper powder.

Pick a special spot to picnic.
Pick a special spot to picnic.
Pick a special spot to picnic.

Pointy pencil points poke at pulpy paper pads.
Pointy pencil points poke at pulpy paper pads.
Pointy pencil points poke at pulpy paper pads.

Pros prefer proper putters.
Pros prefer proper putters.
Pros prefer proper putters.

Pop a tin or trim a pop.
Pop a tin or trim a pop.
Pop a tin or trim a pop.

Preposterous apostrophes.
Preposterous apostrophes.
Preposterous apostrophes.

Pro players peel pale pears.
Pro players peel pale pears.
Pro players peel pale pears.

Puffy hippo pillow.
Puffy hippo pillow.
Puffy hippo pillow.

The quack quit asking quick questions.

The queen coined quick clipped quips.

Quick kiss.
Quick kiss.
Quick kiss.

Quakes cause cracks.

Quincey! Quack quietly or quit quacking!

A right-handed fellow named Wright, in writing "write" always wrote "rite" where he meant to write right. If he'd written "write" right, Wright would not have wrought rot writing "rite."

A well-read redhead.

Rita repeated what Reardon recited when Reardon read the remarks.

The renter refused to remit the rent until a roofer removed the rotten wood from the rotten roof.

Russ removes rust from wristwatches. He's Russ, the wristwatch rust remover.

The right rear wheel on Willy's rally racer won't roll well.

Ray's runway runs one way.

Rhoda raised red roses. Wanda raised white roses.

Richard whined when his wet wristwatch rusted.

Remove the raw rice. Once the raw rice is removed, roast the white rice.

Rigid wicker rockers.

Reed rode in the red wagon when he went to Reagan's. Reed's road was rough, so Reed refused a return ride in the red wagon.

Rival river runners rode the wild river.

Round and round the rugged rocks the ragged rascal ran.

Rex wrecks wet rocks.

Robin robs wealthy widows.

The rhino wore a white ribbon. The white ribbon is what the rhino wore.

If rustlers wrestle wrestlers, While rustlers rustle rustlers, Could rustlers rustle wrestlers While wrestlers wrestle rustlers?

Really rich roaches wear wristwatches.

Ronald won't roll around the round roller rink.

Rough rural roads.
Rough rural roads.
Rough rural roads.

Ruth rowed as Roth rode in the rowboat. Roth refused to row. It was rude of Roth to ride without rowing, while Ruth rowed as she rode with Roth.

The right fruit is ripe fruit.

Raise Ruth's red roof.
Raise Ruth's red roof.
Raise Ruth's red roof.

Rush the washing, Russell!

Really rotten writing.

Rich, ripe, red, raw raisins.

Ron won't run while Wayne runs. Why won't Ron run while Wayne runs? Wayne ruined Ron's new Reboks. "Wayne's to blame," claims Ron.

Reverend Welch recommended wide record racks.

Rudolf resented Ryan's relentless rudeness.

Ray's wife raised rice. The rice Ray's wife raised was wild rice.

Red wrens' wings.
Red wrens' wings.
Red wrens' wings.

Real rear wheels.
Real rear wheels.
Real rear wheels.

Six small slick seals.
Six small slick seals.
Six small slick seals.

Seth's sharp spacesuit shrank.

"Stay seated, Stephanie,"
Stephen said.

Sherman shops at cheap chop
suey shops.

Mrs. Smith's Fish Sauce Shop.

Is Sherry's shortcake shop shut?
Is Shelly's shortstop shop shut?

She sells Swiss sweets.

Six crisp snacks.
Six crisp snacks.
Six crisp snacks.

Sneers and snarls and snail snips.

Stacey Street tasted the tasty treats. The treats tasted tasty to Stacey.

Are the soup and stew through?
The soup's through, but the stew's glue.

Sixteen slim, silky slippers.
Sixteen slim, silky slippers.
Sixteen slim, silky slippers.

Something stinks and I think what stinks are the things in the sink.

Sheila seldom sells shelled shrimps.

She sells seashells by the seashore.

Selfish sharks sell shut shellfish.

Spicy fish sauce.

Stacks of salty snacks make Sam slurp and smack.

Spike spillled the special sauce.

The stinky socks are soaking in the soap in the sink.
If the socks still stink after soaking, sit them in the steamer.
After soaking and steaming, the stinky socks should
smell super.

Stanley Steele still thinks someone stole his smooth steel
sling shot.

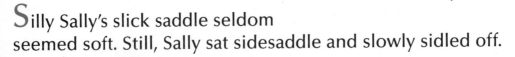

Sally Stiller saddled six sorrel
stallions.

Silly Sally's slick saddle seldom
seemed soft. Still, Sally sat sidesaddle and slowly sidled off.

Susie's shirt shop sells
preshrunk shirts.

Slick silk.
Slick silk.
Slick silk.

Short swords.
Short swords.
Short swords.

Sharon sews shocking shirts for soldiers.

The sad soldier should shoot soon.

Sharpshooters should shoot slowly.

Soldiers' shoulders shudder when shrill shells shriek.

Should six shaking soldiers share the shattered shield?

The short soldier shoots straight.

Sixty-six sick six-shooters.

Stagecoach stops.
Stagecoach stops.
Stagecoach stops.

Strange strategic statistics.
Strange strategic statistics.
Strange strategic statistics.

Soft, smooth snake skin.

The spunky skunk slumped and the stinky slug slouched.
Soon they switched and the spunky skunk slouched and the
stinky slug slumped.

Small, smart snakes
smelling smoked steaks.

How many slim, slimy
snakes would slither
silently to the sea
if slim, slimy snakes
could slither silently?

"Shoot, Sally!" shouted Slim Sam.

Stu's shoe was in Sue's stew.

Are Stan's scuffed snowshoes stuck in the snowy slush?

Sue saw Sam Sawyer sawing cedar shavings.
Sue said, "Stop sawing, Sam," and Sam Sawyer stopped.

Mr. See and Mr. Soar were old friends. See owned a saw and Soar owned a seesaw. Now See's saw sawed Soar's seesaw before Soar saw See, which made Soar sore. Had Soar seen See's saw before See saw Soar's seesaw, then See's saw would not have sawed Soar's seesaw. But See saw Soar's seesaw before Soar saw See's saw, so See's saw sawed Soar's seesaw. It was a shame to let See see Soar so sore, because See's saw sawed Soar's seesaw.

No shipshape ships shop stocks shop-soiled shirts.

"Sure the ship's ship-shape, sir!"

Shallow sailing ships should shun shallow shoals.

The shallow ship showed signs of sinking.

The ship's ceiling was so soaked and soiled, the sailor had to seal the soiled ceiling with ceiling sealer.

Sixty-four swift sloops swing shorewards.

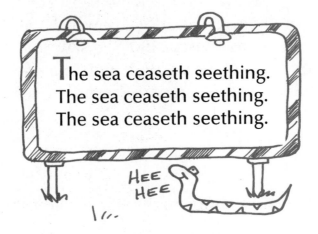

The sea ceaseth seething.
The sea ceaseth seething.
The sea ceaseth seething.

Of all the smells I ever smelt,
I never smelt a smell that smelt
Like that smell I smelt smelled.

A selfish shellfish smelt a
stale fish.
If the stale fish was a smelt,
then the selfish shellfish
smelt a smelt.

Should a shad selling shrimps for a shark,
Cease to shuck the shamed shrimps, who remark,
"Serve us not without dressing! 'Tis really distressing!"
Or should he just shuck the shrimps in the dark?

No shark shares swordfish
steak.

Steffie strained stew through the soup strainer.

"Swim, Sam, swim,
Show them you're a swimmer!
Six sharp sharks seek small snacks,
So swim, Sam, swim!

Swan swam over the sea.
"Swim, Swan, Swim!"
Swan swam back again;
"Well swum, Swan!"

Some say shy shippers
ship shy sheep.

Six sly shavers sheared six shy sheep.

Shameless shepherds
shampoo shy sheep.

Six sick shorn sheep.

The sixth sheik's sixth
sheep's sick.

Shorn sheep shouldn't sleep in a shack.
Shorn sheep should sleep in a shed.

The shady shoe shop shows sharp sharkskin shoes.

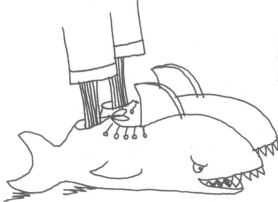

Sharp sharkskin shoes.
Sharp sharkskin shoes.
Sharp sharkskin shoes.

Sid's shabby silver shoes still shine.

Sooty Sukey Shook some soot
From sister Susie's Sooty shoes.

The shrewd shrew's suede shoes.

Steph's stock of stacked soccer
socks stinks.

Shoes and socks shock Susan.

The suitor wore shorts and a short shooting suit to
a short shoot.
But the shorts didn't suit the short shooting suit,
and at the short shoot, the short shooting suit didn't suit.
Oh, shoot!

Six snakes sniffed six sticks.
The snakes sniffed so softly that their sniffing seemed silent.
Soon their soft sniffing stopped.
Then the six snakes that sniffed the six sticks
simply slithered away.

I went into my garden to
slay snails.
I saw my little sister slaying
snails.
I said, "Hello, my little sister,
are you slaying snails?
If you slay snails, please slay small snails."

Sal's sign said, "Small snails for sale." "Sal's small snails smell stale," Sid said.

Sally Swim saw Sadie Slee
Slowly, sadly swinging.
"She seems sorrowful," said she.
So she started singing.
Sadie smiled, soon swiftly swung;
Sitting straight, steered swiftly.
"See," said Sally, "something sung
Scatters sunshine swiftly!"

Surely the sun shall shine soon.

Some shun summer sunshine.

Shirley Simms shrewdly shuns sunshine and sleet.

Sally studied stenciling.

Stupid Stanley Sands stifled Steven Stubbs.

Sue sucks sugar and sherbet through a straw.

Sixty shifty shoplifters shoplifting on a nifty ship.

The sun shines on the shop signs.

Shabby soldiers shovel soft snow slowly.

Sloppy skiers slide on slick ski slopes.

Sneak-thieves seized the skis.

Sleepy Joe of snowy Stowe slid swiftly into action. Aboard his sled away he sped. He's sleeping now, in traction.

Seven sleek sleepless sleepers seek sleep.

The slightly sloping shed slips.

The shaky shed sheds
sheets of shale.

Sick cattle slip on slick
ski slopes.

If he slipped, should she slip?

Is there a strap on the cap on the chap?
Or is there no strap on the cap on the chap?

Sloppy shortstops.
Sloppy shortstops.
Sloppy shortstops.

The sly sheet slasher slashed sheets.

Sixty-six sticky skeletons.
Sixty-six sticky skeletons.
Sixty-six sticky skeletons.

She shall sew a slit sheet shut.

A ghost's sheets would soon shrink in such suds.

She shrieks as she stitches sheets.

Should she sell sheer sheets or should she sell shaggy shawls?

Amidst the mists and coldest frosts,
With barest wrists and stoutest boasts,
He thrusts his fists against the posts,
And still insists he sees the ghosts.

Some say Seymour saw more, but Seymour won't say more.
"Saw what you saw, Seymour!" some shouted.

Sally sells soil samples at the soil store.
Sometimes there are seashells in the soil samples Sally sells.

"Go, my son, and shut the shutter."
This I heard a mother mutter.
"Shutter's shut," the boy did mutter,
"I can't shut'er any shutter."

Should she shut summer
shutters slowly or should she
shut summer shutters swiftly?

It is so chilly, the silly child should soon shut the shutters.

Steven Stanley sees seven stars.

Does someone know a synonym
for cinnamon?
Someone once said that cinnamon
has no synonym.
But surely there must be a synonym
for cinnamon.

Tongue Twisters –S–

Shouldn't sweet-scented shaving soap soothe sore skin?

If silly Sally will shilly-shally, shall silly Willy willy-nilly shilly-shally, too?

A skunk sat on a stump. The skunk thunk the stump stunk, But the stump thunk the skunk stunk.

Shawn shaves a short cedar shingle thin.

Sad skunk.
Sad skunk.
Sad skunk.

Should Shawn shave a short, thin, single cedar shingle thin, or shave a short, thin, single, cedar shingle thinner?

I had an old saw, and I bought a new saw. I took the handle off the sold saw and put it on the new saw. And of all the saws I ever saw, I never saw a saw saw like that new saw sawed.

Some slow sloths sleep soundly. Some slow sloths snore strongly.

Sissy saw some simple thimbles.

Shirley showed Cher some chairs she sewed.

Sid's sister assisted Sissy.

Sharon sewed six shiny suits.

Suzie's sister saw some scissors Suzie set on her sofa.

Mr. Spink thinks the sphinx stinks.

Scott's skate slipped as Scott skated. "I think I'll skip these slippery skates," Scott said.

Sarah Sawyer sold several soldiers sodas.

Sarah slurped soda through straight, striped soda straws.

Several nervous servers spilled slops.

Several silly servers served Sally squash soup.

Stewart soon stopped sniffing the stinky stuff Sandy stirred with the stick.

I love tongue twisters that start with the letter sssss . . .

Does this shop stock shot silk shorts?

If she stops at the shop where I stop, and if she shops at the shop where I shop, then I shan't stop at the shop where she stops to shop.

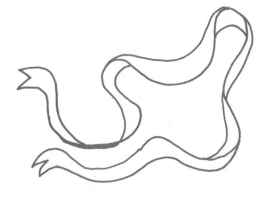

Showy sashes in a shut sash shop.

Such a shapeless sash!
Such a shapeless sash!
Such a shapeless sash!

The shepherd swiftly sheared the sleepy sheep with the sharp scissors.

Sue sure seems scared of school.

The old school scold
Sold the school coal scuttle;
If the old school scold sold
The school coal scutle,
The school should scold
And scuttle the old school scold.

"What a strange stain," stated Stan. That stain was the strangest stain Stan said he'd seen.

Sy's son shines signs and sighs shyly.

Stan stopped stealing Sam's stamps.

Chester Sutter just suggested Jess test Esther's chess set.

Mrs. Swister kissed her sister's blister.

I snuff shop snuff. Do you snuff shop snuff?

Sal served Saul some sour soy sauce.

Sometimes Sheila thinks such soft thoughts.

Down the slippery slide they slid, sitting slightly sideways; slipping swiftly, see them skid on holidays and Fridays.

Scams, stings, and skulduggery.
Scams, stings, and skulduggery.
Scams, stings, and skulduggery.

"Stow your snowshoes, Sue."

Sally sipped a saucer of simmering soup.
Sally sipped a saucer of simmering soup.
Sally sipped a saucer of simmering soup.

Sally slapped a silly salmon.
Sally slapped a silly salmon.
Sally slapped a silly salmon.

Saw you sawing Suzy's seesaw!
Saw you sawing Suzy's seesaw!
Saw you sawing Suzy's seesaw!

Say, what a shame the game's a sham.
Say, what a shame the game's a sham.
Say, what a shame the game's a sham.

Seven sailboats steered with sextants.
Seven sailboats steered with sextants.
Seven sailboats steered with sextants.

Several similar symbols.
Several similar symbols.
Several similar symbols.

She says she saw it.
She says she saw it.
She says she saw it.

She should say she's sorry.
She should say she's sorry.
She should say she's sorry.

She shouldn't stow such showy shoes, should she?
She shouldn't stow such showy shoes, should she?
She shouldn't stow such showy shoes, should she?

She sneezes, sways, and snores and swoons.
She sneezes, sways, and snores and swoons.
She sneezes, sways, and snores and swoons.

She wished her sister pushed us swifter.
She wished her sister pushed us swifter.
She wished her sister pushed us swifter.

Sheila shined her sister's silver.
Sheila shined her sister's silver.
Sheila shined her sister's silver.

Sherrie sports a silly sort of shorts.
Sherrie sports a silly sort of shorts.
Sherrie sports a silly sort of shorts.

Shoddy, soggy shoes.
Shoddy, soggy shoes.
Shoddy, soggy shoes.

Silken satin sequined soccer shorts.
Silken satin sequined soccer shorts.
Silken satin sequined soccer shorts.

Silly Stanley sampled stinky Stilton.
Silly Stanley sampled stinky Stilton.
Silly Stanley sampled stinky Stilton.

Simon's stumped. Send Stan a simpler sample.
Simon's stumped. Send Stan a simpler sample.
Simon's stumped. Send Stan a simpler sample.

Simply sipping supper slowly.
Simply sipping supper slowly.
Simply sipping supper slowly.

Someone won some sum, son!
Someone won some sum, son!
Someone won some sum, son!

Sport something simple and stylish.
Sport something simple and stylish.
Sport something simple and stylish.

Stella stuck several sticky stamps.
Stella stuck several sticky stamps.
Stella stuck several sticky stamps.

Stunned, Stan stood stock still.
Stunned, Stan stood stock still.
Stunned, Stan stood stock still.

Such a shame to see such shortages!
Such a shame to see such shortages!
Such a shame to see such shortages!

Sue's shoes sure sound squeaky!
Sue's shoes sure sound squeaky!
Sue's shoes sure sound squeaky!

Summer summons some surfers!
Summer summons some surfers!
Summer summons some surfers!

Sure, she's shy, so she stays inside.
Sure, she's shy, so she stays inside.
Sure, she's shy, so she stays inside.

Surely she was sorry she spoke so scandalously of Shirley!
Surely she was sorry she spoke so scandalously of Shirley!
Surely she was sorry she spoke so scandalously of Shirley!

Susie's super applesauce.
Susie's super applesauce.
Susie's super applesauce.

Sweet cinnamon sediment.
Sweet cinnamon sediment.
Sweet cinnamon sediment.

A tutor who tooted a flute
tried to tutor two tooters
to toot.
Said the two to the tutor,
"Is it harder to toot or to
tutor two tooters to toot?"

Timothy tapped on the tympani.

I thought a thought.
But the thought I thought
I thought wasn't the thought
I thought.
If the thought I thought had been
the thought I thought I thought,
I wouldn't have thought so much.

Do thick tinkers think?

There goes one tough top cop!
There goes one tough top cop!
There goes one tough top cop!

Tea for the thin twin tinsmith.

That's Tim's stack of tin thumbtacks.

Thick ticks think thin ticks are sick.

The throne was frozen. It was a frozen throne.

Thirteen drummers thumping drums.
Thirteen drummers thumping drums.
Thirteen drummers thumping drums.

Thistle thorns stick.

It took Tom time to try to tote two totems to town.

Two ticket takers took a taxi.
Two ticket takers took a taxi.
Two ticket takers took a taxi.

WE'VE GOT THE TICKETS... LET'S GO!

TAXI

Twelve tiny thread tweezers.
Twelve tiny thread tweezers.
Twelve tiny thread tweezers.

Twenty tender tree stumps.
Twenty tender tree stumps.
Twenty tender tree stumps.

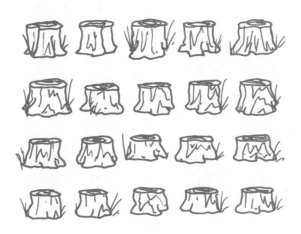

He says that a two twice-twisted twine twisted twice twists twice as tight as a one once-twisted twine twisted twice. But I say that a two twice-twisted twine twisted twice does not twist as tight as a one once-twisted twine twisted twice.

The tailor's tactics took twice the time.

Three thrushes rush thusly.

She shot three shy thrushes.

Thirty-three sly shy thrushes.
Thirty-three sly shy thrushes.
Thirty-three sly shy thrushes.

Theophilus Thistle, the successful thistle-sifter,
Sifted sixty thistles through the thick of his thumb.

Thick thistle sticks.
Thick thistle sticks.
Thick thistle sticks.

Six thick thistles stuck together.

Trent ties Ty's ties to trees to trick Ty.

Ted sent Stan ten tents.

A tree toad loved a she-toad
That lived up in a tree.
She was a three-toed tree toad,
But a two-toed toad was he.
The two-toed toad tried to win
The she-toad's friendly nod,
For the two-toed toad loved the
ground
On which the three-toed tree toad trod.
But no matter how the two-toed tree toad tried,
He could not please her whim.
In her three-toed bower,
With her three-toed power,
The three-toed she-toad vetoed him.

Ted threw Fred thirty-three free throws.

Three thick things
Three thick things.
Three thick things.

Three free through trains.
Three free through trains.
Three free through trains.

Truly rural.
Truly rural.
Truly rural.

Twixt six thick thumbs stick six thick sticks.

Tim and Tom taped two tom-toms together. Then Tim and Tom tapped the tom-toms. Today, Tim's Mom tapped the tom-toms too. But Tom's Mom thought all that tom-tom tapping was terrible.

Turtles waddle. Waiters toddle.

Tacky tractor trailer trucks.
Tacky tractor trailer trucks.
Tacky tractor trailer trucks.

Trill two true tunes to the troops.

Theo's throat throbs and thumps, thumps and throbs.

Thelma sings the theme song.

Twelve trim twin-track tapes.
Twelve trim twin-track tapes.
Twelve trim twin-track tapes.

Tabby tested ten tempting tins of tuna.
Tabby tested ten tempting tins of tuna.
Tabby tested ten tempting tins of tuna.

Thaw those three frozen toes.
Thaw those three frozen toes.
Thaw those three frozen toes.

They threw the thing they think they threw.
They threw the thing they think they threw.
They threw the thing they think they threw.

Ten toasts for the tense hoast whose hens we tasted and roast we ate.
Ten toasts for the tense hoast whose hens we tasted and roast we ate.
Ten toasts for the tense hoast whose hens we tasted and roast we ate.

They've seen three thieves leave the scene!
They've seen three thieves leave the scene!
They've seen three thieves leave the scene!

Thick as three tricky thieves.
Thick as three tricky thieves.
Thick as three tricky thieves.

Tina's toddler's too much trouble.
Tina's toddler's too much trouble.
Tina's toddler's too much trouble.

Treacherous Trevor tracked trout.
Treacherous Trevor tracked trout.
Treacherous Trevor tracked trout.

Trolls toil in dungeons.
Trolls toil in dungeons.
Trolls toil in dungeons.

An undertaker undertook to undertake an undertaking.
The undertaking that the undertaker undertook was the hardest undertaking the undertaker ever undertook to undertake.

Underwood would wear underwear if Underwood knew where his underwear was.
Underwood's underwear was in Durwood's woods.
Underwood went into Durwood's woods and got his underwear.

Unique New York.
Unique New York.
Unique New York.

The U.S. twin-screw cruiser.
The U.S. twin-screw cruiser.
The U.S. twin-screw cruiser.

Unsung songs.
Unsung songs.
Unsung songs.

What veteran ventriloquist whistles?

Valuable valley villas.
Valuable valley villas.
Valuable valley villas.

The vicious visitors
visited the virtual village.

Grrr...

Vandals waxed Valerie's white van.

The wretched witch watched a walrus washing.
Did the wretched witch watch a walrus washing?
If the wretched witch watched a walrus washing,
Where's the washing walrus the wretched witch watched?

An itchy rich witch.

Which switch is the witch's switch?

If two witches watched two watches, which witch would watch which watch?

These witch twisters have
twisted this witch.

Real wristwatch straps.
Real wristwatch straps.
Real wristwatch straps.

Which wristwatch is a Swiss wristwatch?

I wish I hadn't washed this wristwatch.
I washed all the wheels and the works.
Since this wristwatch got all washed,
Oh, how it jumps and jerks!

Wire rimmed wheels.

Wyatt wondered why the worn
wires weren't wrapped right.

How much wood would a woodchuck chuck if a woodchuck could chuck wood?
He would chuck the wood as much as he could if a woodchuck could chuck wood.

Whether the weather be fine
Or whether the weather be not;
Whether the weather be cold
Or whether the weather be hot;
We'll weather the weather
Whatever the weather,
Whether we like it or not.

Wee Willie Winkie risks three wishes.

White wings, round rings.
White wings, round rings.
White wings, round rings.

Wild wrens wing westward.

When Dwight White writes,
Dwight writes right.

Will won't write a real will.

Wally Wrinkle wriggles
his white, wrinkled wig.

One really wet red whale.

Wallie wrecked Randy's railway.

Weary railroad workers.

We walruses won't wear winter wool in warm weather.
We walruses won't wear winter wool in warm weather.
We walruses won't wear winter wool in warm weather.

We watched the walrus washing.
We watched the walrus washing.
We watched the walrus washing.

We won when we wore our armor!
We won when we wore our armor!
We won when we wore our armor!

We'll wheel right when the wheelwright rears.
We'll wheel right when the wheelwright rears.
We'll wheel right when the wheelwright rears.

What a way to wake a
weary waiter!
What a way to wake a
weary waiter!
What a way to wake a
weary waiter!

What way were we when we went way wrong?
What way were we when we went way wrong?
What way were we when we went way wrong?

When walking west, one rarely wanders.
When walking west, one rarely wanders.
When walking west, one rarely wanders.

When you wind twine, mind your behind is not intertwined in the line that you wind.

Which rich witch went every which way?
Which rich witch went every which way?
Which rich witch went every which way?

Whistle with a little lisp!
Whistle with a little lisp!
Whistle with a little lisp!

Xmas wrecks perplex and vex.

X-ray checks clear chests.

Ex-disk jockey.
Ex-disk jockey.
Ex-disk jockey.

The ex-egg examiner.
The ex-egg examiner.
The ex-egg examiner.

Agnes' "X"s are excellent. Agnes excels in executing "X"s.

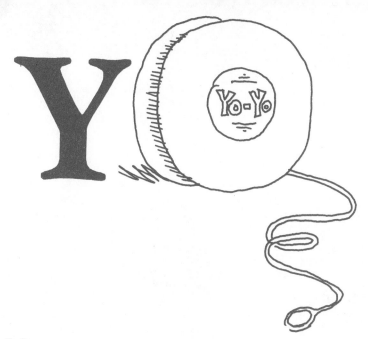

Yanking yellow yo-yos.
Yanking yellow yo-yos.
Yanking yellow yo-yos.

Yellow leather, red feather.
Yellow leather, red feather.
Yellow leather, red feather.

Local yokel jokes.
Local yokel jokes.
Local yokel jokes.

Yesterday Yolanda yelled at Euwell.
Usually, Yuri yells at Euwell.

This is a zither.
Is this a zither?

This is Zoe's sister's zither.

Zithers slither slowly south.

Zizzi's zippy zipper zips.

Zack's backpack lacks Zach's snacks.

INDEX

ILLUSTRATION CREDITS